THE ETRUSCANS

THE APOLLO OF VEII

THE ETRUSCANS

By DAVID RANDALL-MACIVER

OXFORD MCMXXVII
AT THE CLARENDON PRESS

PRINTED IN ENGLAND AT THE
UNIVERSITY PRESS, OXFORD
BY JOHN JOHNSON
PRINTER TO THE UNIVERSITY

CONTENTS

LIST OF ILLUSTRATIONS

CHAPTER 1

Ruskin's opinion ; Why the Etruscans are interesting ; Continuity of life and character in Tuscany ; Extent of Etruscan domination ; Untrustworthiness of literary evidence ; Origin according to Herodotus ; Untenable theories of other writers as to origin ; The Etruscans were immigrants from Asia Minor ; Date and manner of their arrival ; Derivation of the name ; Possible connexion with Tursha.

THERE are few people to whom it would be quite a natural thing to go on the first day after their arrival in Florence to the Museo Archeologico. It seems to have so little to do with all the varied interests and enthusiasms which have brought them to Italy. They have come here to live again in the glorious days of the Middle Ages and the Renaissance, to see the works of Giotto and Donatello and Michelangelo, to wander and dream in the streets where Dante trod. Very early in his pilgrimage, therefore, the ardent lover of art will no doubt wend his way to the cloisters of Santa Maria Novella and open the well-known pages of his *Mornings in Florence*. But there, perhaps, some passages in that classic homily will strike him with sudden force. He may be surprised to realize that Ruskin lays great stress on the *Etruscan* origin and descent of the great Florentine painters : ' Central stood Etruscan Florence . . . Child of her peace

B

and exponent of her passion, her Cimabue . . .'
Or again : ' Cimabue, Etruscan-born gave . . .
eager action to holy contemplation.'

This may lead to reflection. Our pioneer teacher
in Italian art is declaring that the Etruscans are
not a mere phantom of the past, is stating that they
have played an important part in the formation of
the Italy that we love. It must be worth while,
then, to know more about them. Ancient history
is baffling and contradictory, but out of all the
myths and legends and poetic distortions certain
facts stand out clearly. It is plain, for instance,
that the Etruscans were once the most important
people in all Italy, and that they did more than
any others to mould its civilization. The Romans
themselves owed much of their religion and much
of their political, social, and military organization
to the Etruscans. Moreover, when they conquered
Central and Northern Italy the Romans found it
permeated all through with a very advanced civilization, which they themselves could never have
produced, though they were fortunate enough to
inherit it—and this civilization was the work of the
Etruscans.

Ruskin, with the insight of a great critic, has
divined rightly when he suggests that to appreciate
the work of a fourteenth-century painter in Tuscany we must study his history and origins, the

soil and the race from which he springs. More than two thousand years of continuous development had gone to the making of Giotto and his school. They did not spring fully armed from the head of any Byzantine; many centuries of thought and observation and study had unconsciously prepared their birth. So it was also with their mightier successors; not only Dante but even Michelangelo owes the possibility of his existence to an Etruscan ancestry, spiritual as well as physical. It was by no mere accident that Niccolò Pisano, the earliest of the great sculptors, found his first models in the old sarcophagi of the Campo Santo at Pisa. He was really discovering his own parentage and returning to the natural inspiration of his race. Often we may think that the earliest work of the Pisani and the drawings of Giotto's pupils repeat mannerisms peculiar to Etruscan sculpture and painting, but, if so, these are only the superficial expression of a spiritual identity which goes far deeper. The temperament and outlook of any Tuscan artist in the Middle Ages or the Renaissance are directly inherited from a long line of ancestors, whose works are to be seen in such places as the Museo Archeologico. It is, therefore, no dry or dusty study into which I would lure the reader; on the contrary it is a subject which lies at the core of everything which interests him as well as me, in the city of Florence and the work of her greatest men.

The continuity of life and customs in Tuscany is very remarkable, and very important to understand. All the changes and chances of history have left this heart of Central Italy essentially the same that it has been for about three thousand years. Never swamped by any foreign invasion the race has remained unchanged. Just as you may recognize to-day in the streets of Florence the living replicas of men and women painted by Ghirlandajo, so you must realize that pictures of the fourteenth and fifteenth centuries are made by the lineal descendants of those who frescoed the walls of their rock-tombs in Etruria centuries before the birth of Christ.

Even in externals there are many obvious survivals. The loggia of a modern Tuscan house finds its precise equivalent in models carved in stone about 400 B.C. Work in the fields and vineyards is little different from what it was when the Etruscans planted the olives and introduced the vine. The *stornelli*, those improvised epigrams which the labourers fling at one another or at the bystander as they till the soil, are only modern equivalents of the Fescennine verses mentioned by Horace. Even in the folklore and superstitions of the country-side there may linger faint reminis-

cences of deities dethroned; the red-capped goblin
of the peasant is perhaps an Etruscan god. Sometimes I even think that the rough aspirations of the
lingua toscana, which are like the burr of our own
north-countrymen compared to the softer accents
of other provinces, may be inherited from the pre-
Italian language with its notoriously harsh consonants.

The territory of the Etruscans once extended
over a far wider range than modern Tuscany.
'The renown of their name', says Livy, 'filled the
whole length of Italy from the Alps to the Sicilian
strait.' Other ancient writers confirm this statement which might otherwise have been discounted
as a rhetorical exaggeration. And though there
is no evidence that their influence ever really extended as far as Calabria, yet archaeology and
history are fully agreed that it can be traced as far
south as Naples, and as far north as the borders of
Switzerland and Austria. The time of the greatest
political power of the Etruscans was just about
500 B.C. In the next century it was undermined
and began to collapse, owing to causes which will
be detailed in my later chapters. By the time of
the early Roman Empire Etruria had come to
mean almost the same as modern Tuscany, except
that its southern boundary was the Tiber, and
that it included a part of Umbria.

Curiously enough there has never been any written history of the Etruscans. It is said that the Emperor Claudius, who was a literary man of the same sort of calibre as our own James the First of England, composed a history in some twenty books; but it may be doubted whether we have lost much real knowledge by its disappearance. For, as it seems that there was no native historian on whom he could build, the voluminous work must have been little more than a farrago of the tales invented by jealous Greeks, who had a strong personal interest in manufacturing propaganda for their own glorification. Most of the Greek pedigrees and stories of early settlement, as well as the slanderous comments on Etruscan life and manners, are deliberate attempts to poison the wells of truth. Nor are the Latin writers of the Augustan period, even Livy and Vergil, to be trusted. They lived centuries later than the great days of Etruria, so that they had no real sources of information ; and it was the policy of their time to glorify the Romans at the expense of all others. Vergil is admittedly writing a romance, his Mezentius of Caere is an invention; Livy is interested only in telling the story of Roman achievement to which the Etruscans are a mere background. At most we get some picture of their military strength and tenacity from the narrative of long wars and sieges.

All that we know of the origins, art, or civilization of the Etruscans is due almost entirely to archaeology. It is due to the excavations and studies which have been made for many years in the *Cities and Cemeteries of Etruria*, to quote the apt title of that delightful classic which was written by one of our own countrymen, George Dennis, in the middle of the nineteenth century. What I have to tell, then, in this volume will be based almost wholly on archaeological evidence, not upon any attempt to weave a coherent whole out of the patchwork of fragments embedded in obscure Latin and Greek commentators, or the biased references which occur incidentally in the works of the classical poets and historians.

There is, however, one important point upon which literary evidence may be taken into account, though I should not have emphasized the literary tradition if it had not been fully corroborated by archaeology. Herodotus has given us a story of Etruscan origins which has been scoffed at by over-ingenious writers of the schools of Niebuhr and Mommsen, but has lately won the almost unreserved support of the best scholars in Italy and France and Germany and England. His tale, of which the minor details are unessential, relates how once in a time of famine a number of inhabitants of Lydia in Asia Minor decided to emigrate and followed one of the sons of their king to the country of the Ombrikoi. By Ombrikoi he means, like all Greek writers, the Umbrians, who according to tradition once occupied a much larger part of Italy than the modern province of that name. The Lydians settled among them and called themselves Tyrsenoi after the name of the prince who led them.

This story was almost universally accepted in antiquity and is found in every poet or prose-writer except Dionysius. There are some picturesque illustrations of it. Plutarch, for instance, relates that in memory of the victory over Veii the Romans used to lead round at their official triumphs an old man dressed in the Etruscan toga and bulla, while a herald shouted derisively 'Sardians to sell'. Again, when a deputation from Sardis was competing with other cities for the honour of dedicating a temple to Tiberius, its members quoted a decree of the Etruscan confederacy rehearsing the genealogy given by Herodotus.

The unanimity of all ancient writers except one is not, of course, really valuable as evidence. They may all have been echoing the same original authority. This is the reason that modern critics have thought that Dionysius of Halicarnassus, though alone in his opinion, is as valuable as the whole mass of other classical authorities who are against him. This Greek, who wrote his *Roman*

Archaeology in the time of Augustus, no doubt supposed himself to be something of an original authority because he was born in Asia Minor. He was piqued by the universal respect shown to Herodotus, and tried to set up against him the authority of a Lydian writer of the fifth century, one Xanthus. But he had not a copy of Xanthus to work from, nothing better than a *réchauffé* made as late as the third century B.C., regarded by some scholars of the time as an actual forgery. But even if we accept the writings of Xanthus as genuine we shall find that the deductions which Dionysius draws from them are quite unsound. Merely because Xanthus omits to mention the emigration of the Tyrsenoi we are asked to believe that it cannot have taken place. It is the weakest form of argument *ex silentio* that was ever put forward.

As a corollary of his denial that the Etruscans came from Lydia Dionysius maintains that they must have been autochthonous, that is to say, sprung from the soil of Italy itself. It is a theory which one or two modern historians have tried to revive, but always without success because the obvious and fatal objection to it is that the language, according to Dionysius' own statement, is wholly peculiar and unlike that of any other people in Italy. Had the Etruscans been related to any of the original inhabitants they must have spoken some one of the languages which were still used in the days of Dionysius by the descendants of the Stone Age and Bronze Age people in Italy. These descendants were surviving all over the country in the time of Augustus, and were speaking many different dialects, but they were all dialects of the same family. The strangeness of their speech shows that the Etruscans were strangers.

A more plausible theory, which was generally held through the nineteenth century, and has only recently been exploded by archaeological research, was that of the great German historian Niebuhr. He supposed that some traces of the Etruscan language still lingered in the valleys of the Eastern Alps, and in spite of Livy's direct statement that the people of those valleys were degenerate fugitives who had gone wild in their savage surroundings, he maintained that they were the surviving descendants of an original invading army which had come over the Alps in prehistoric days.

There are such numerous objections of every kind to this view, it is so inadequate to explain any of the facts, and rests to begin with on such a flimsy foundation of philological hypothesis, that it is surprising to find that it has been so widely accepted. Fortunately, it has been positively disproved by explorations made in and around Bologna, which was the site of the Etruscan city of

Felsina. It has been shown that Felsina, the principal town of the whole region, was not founded until the end of the sixth century B.C., and that nowhere north of the Apennines is there a single Etruscan colony of any earlier date. Consequently, as the most obstinate theorists would hardly dare to maintain that the Etruscans arrived in Italy for the first time as late as 500 B.C., the very date in fact when the Tarquins were being expelled from Rome, it is evident that Niebuhr's theory must be finally abandoned.

I shall return in a later chapter to the subject of the excavations at Bologna, which were extremely important for many reasons. They showed a perfectly clear-cut division between the settlements of the Etruscan colonists and those of their Italian predecessors.

It may be said, then, that all the theories which have been put forward in contradiction to Herodotus have totally failed, and that there is no inherent reason why the tradition which he records should not be accepted, at least in its broad lines. To this it must now be added that the immigration of the Etruscans from Asia Minor, if not actually from Lydia which is a matter of less importance, offers a perfect explanation of all the facts revealed by exploration. For we now know a great deal as to the relative antiquity of the different Etruscan sites in Italy, and the striking thing that appears is that without exception the oldest are on the sea-coast. All the inland cities, though often on sites which had long previously been inhabited by the Italians, are of distinctly later foundation. The original cities are Tarquinia, Caere, and Vetulonia, situated on that strip of sea-coast which is called the Tuscan Maremma.

It is easy to guess the motive which brought these sea wanderers from Asia to the western coasts of Italy, if we remember what were the principal interests and needs of a people living a little after the time of Homer. Copper was the most important of all commodities, necessary above all for weapons, and copper was common in Tuscany, where the natives had already worked it for several centuries. Iron was just coming into use, and iron is particularly abundant in the island of Elba, just opposite the very point which the Etruscans chose for their landing-parties. North of the Apennines iron is quite rare until the period of active intercourse and trade with the western coast. But it is very common all over Etruria from the eighth century downwards, and actually makes its first appearance in any quantity in the earliest years that can be detected as Etruscan.

On a site like Vetulonia, where there is an unbroken continuity of residence beginning with the native Italians and leading on to the Etruscan burials, we can trace the sudden increase in the use of all metals when the Asiatics arrive about 800 B.C. The Italians had worked copper quite freely but their use of iron was very limited. But the new-comers were soon using iron quite prodigally, even for the harness of their horses and the wheels of their chariots. They exploited the mines to the full, and it was their command of all the sources of mineral supply, together with their skill in smelting and forging, which made their military success possible and provided them with the chief sources of their wealth. The Etruscans must have been skilled workers in metal before they left their own homes, as the products of the first generation of immigrants are too fine to have been produced by novices. They were fortunate, however, in finding very apt pupils among the native Italians. These had developed a high standard of work in copper and bronze even without the aid of foreign teachers. They had brought a knowledge of the coppersmith's art from the far-away valley of the Danube, whence they themselves had emigrated two or three centuries before.

From the evidence of the cemeteries the immigration of the Etruscans may be placed about the end of the ninth century. It must not be supposed that they came as a vast conquering host. Rather

it would seem that they arrived in small detachments a few at a time, perhaps just one or two
ships every year. Very probably they had been
exploring all round the Mediterranean for some
generations before they finally decided on the
place where it was most profitable to settle. Some
writers have argued that they would never have
chosen to go so far northward if Campania and
the southern coasts had been open to them, and
from this proceed to reason that the first Greek
colonies must have been earlier. This is quite unnecessary. We might well retort that on the contrary the Greeks would never have failed to choose
Tuscany if it had been open to them to go there.
Actually, of course, there are no traces of Greek
settlement north of Naples, and such stories as
those which make Falerii a Greek city are palpa-
ble inventions of a later age entirely discredited by
archaeology.

The sort of process by which we may suppose
that the Etruscans took gradual possession of the
new country may be illustrated by the periodical
descents of the Northmen on the coasts of Scot-
land, as told in the Icelandic sagas. In any pro-
mising spring season a ship or two might sail from
a port in Asia Minor, carrying one or two families
with their retainers. These would land and en-
trench themselves on a commanding hill like that

of Vetulonia. With their carefully chosen and finely tempered weapons, as important to them as a Norman's great sword and perhaps quite as effective, they would maintain their ground against the weaker Italians, and hold their youthful city until the new year, when another band of their friends and relatives might come to join them. The separate cities of Etruria were never united under a single head at any moment in their history, they always formed a rather loose confederation, such as might very naturally exist between independent but related clans. Probably each of the great cities was founded by a separate family or clan, not invariably on perfectly good terms with all the rest. The tie between some cities was much closer than that between others. On occasions of a great emergency, a common danger threatening them all, they might unite. But for the complete gathering of the clans a very great common interest was necessary. I doubt whether Lars Porsenna of Clusium could count on as much allegiance as the head of the house of Argyll, and I am sure that the Macdonalds of Caere were always unreliable.

The Etruscans themselves formed a small and close oligarchy in each city, the real backbone of their power was in the native tribes whom they had subjugated. These Italians of Etruria stood towards the Etruscans much as the Saxons in England stood to their Norman overlords. There are traces here and there of the reciprocal effect of native and foreign customs. If the two races never amalgamated yet they lived on terms of complete harmony forming a series of homogeneous states.

Though composed of so many different units the loosely welded nation was known by a single collective name. To the Greeks of the time of Herodotus they were familiar as Tyrsenoi or Tyrrhenoi. Dionysius said that they called themselves Rasenna after the name of one of their chiefs. We have seen some reason to distrust this author's omniscience, but it does not greatly matter whether he was right or wrong in this particular case, as, though the name of Rasenna is a perfectly correct Etruscan formation, it does not enter into literature. Tyrsenoi and Tyrrhenoi are the words which have left their mark on history. To the latter we owe the name of the Tyrrhenian sea which washes the western coast of Italy, while through Tyrsenoi we have obtained not only the Latin Etrusci but the medieval Tuscia and the modern name of Tuscany.

It is an interesting speculation whether the name Tyrs-enoi, in which the last two syllables seem to be a sort of collective termination often found in Asia Minor, may not be the same as that of Tursha mentioned on Egyptian monuments. These Tursha, allied with two other nations whose names may well be those of Lycians and Achaeans, made a descent on the coasts of Egypt in the thirteenth century B.C. This was, of course, long before the Etruscans had settled in Italy, but if the identification is correct it shows that they were a formidable seafaring people several centuries before they appeared in the West.

IT is interesting to see what these stout sea-rob-
bers looked like. Unfortunately, there are no
pictures or records of their ships, for though some
little models of boats have been found in the tombs
they are only ceremonial or pleasure boats. It is
likely that the Etruscans sailed and rowed in such
small vessels as those described in Homer, which
could be readily pulled up on to the shore. Two
gravestones in the museum at Florence, to be
dated only about two or three generations after the
conquest, give some idea of the dress and equipment of the warriors who landed about 820 B.C. at
Vetulonia and a little farther south near Tarquinia. One of them, roughly incised on soft stone,
shows a man named Avtilés Feluskés armed with
a double axe and a round shield. The other, from
distant Volterra, shows Larthi Atharnies wearing a
dress and buskins of quite Asiatic style, and carrying a curved sword unlike anything that has been
found in the tombs.

As time went on the Etruscan fighting force became very highly organized. The cavalry was always formidable, and must have been a favourite corps with a people who were so devoted to horses and horse-racing as their pictures show. There was nothing new about the use of the horse in Italy. Graves at Bologna far earlier than the Etruscan colonization have yielded many examples of bit and bridle. Chariots, however, were unknown until the Etruscans introduced them, when they became an inseparable part of the life of any man of position. Every important grave on some sites contained portions of chariots, made partly of bronze and partly of iron. A nobleman after his death went down to the underworld in his chariot just as an Egyptian was ferried there in a boat.

But the backbone of the army must always have been composed of heavy armed footmen, and it is a fair inference that they were recruited mainly amongst the native Italians. Some very interesting little reliefs, on a bronze vessel of just about 500 B.C., show detachments of the army exactly at the time of its greatest strength and efficiency, when the Etruscan conquests had reached their widest limits. The occasion is a funeral procession, conducted apparently with full military honours, the spearmen bear their weapons point downwards as we should carry our rifles reversed. Led by two mounted men (Plate 1, 1) are five spearmen, carrying oval shields and wearing helmets of a very peculiar form with protuberant knobs. Next to these are four spearmen in crested helmets with quadrangular shields. Then four more with shields of a round form. Finally, there are four men in conical helmets without shields, carrying on their shoulders the wide single axe which is well known from examples found in the tombs. This, then, is a sample of the various divisions of that fighting force which the Romans encountered on many a field, and which actually formed the model of their own army. It is worth remarking on the variety of forms in the helmets and shields. Some are adapted from the Greek, some are only recently borrowed from the Eastern Alps, others again have come down from the first Pilgrim Fathers of the ninth century B.C. The Etruscans were remarkably good learners, they often remind us of the Japanese in their capacity for adaptation. So they borrowed, imported, and applied every modification that might make their army more efficient. Individuals, men of rank who were at liberty to chose their own weapon, would even have one of the spiral-hilted swords from the Danube, a thing as rare and as highly prized as a Toledo blade amongst our own ancestors.

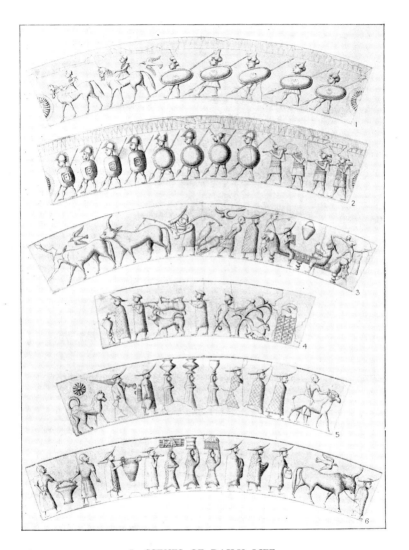

I. SCENES OF DAILY LIFE

From an engraved situla

The same series of little reliefs gives some almost unique representations of country life and village amusements. Here no doubt we may see the Italian of the lower classes, which had become subject to the proud Etruscan nobility, working like our own Saxons after the Norman Conquest peacefully and quietly on their fields. The ploughman (Plate I, 3) has just unyoked his oxen and is resting on his shoulder a little plough which must have been very light, of wood perhaps shod with metal at the tip; next to him a rustic is dragging the carcass of a freshly killed pig on which a bird, perhaps the ominous raven, has perched. In the scene below (Plate I, 4) a hunter wielding a round-headed mace in each hand is driving the hare into a net skilfully prepared to catch it. And on the left of this two men are bearing on two poles the deer just killed in the hunt, while a dog with symmetrically curved tail runs happily underneath it. It might be a scene in the Forest of Arden, and for that matter the forests must have been full of game and wild beasts.

There was an immense work to do in reclaiming the land, which in those days wore a very different aspect from any that we can imagine. Impenetrable woods covered the whole country, broken only here and there by the sparse settlements of the Italians. Nothing could be more unlike the uninterrupted miles of oliveyards, vineyards, and wheatfields which make the beauty and the wealth of modern Tuscany. Directed by their inventive and ingenious lords the Etruscans and Italians drained the marshes, controlled the rivers, and made emissaries for the flooding lakes. They cut the trees to provide furnaces for the smithy, and to obtain timber for the building of their powerful navy. Agriculture was improved, the vine was introduced and widely cultivated, the olive replaced the chestnut and the oak.

But agriculture was by no means the only employment of the people. Arts and crafts, some native and others newly introduced, occupied a large section of the community. The old trade of bronze-working was brought to such a pitch of perfection that even the Greeks recognized the Etruscans as the greatest masters of their time. As early as the seventh century large cauldrons from Vetulonia were actually thought worthy of dedication at Olympia. In the fifth century Etruscan bronze vessels were freely marketed over the Alps to Germany and France. Etruscan goldwork of the seventh century B.C. is certainly the finest found anywhere in the ancient world. Of pottery-making and other crafts I will say something in a later chapter. For the moment my object is only to bring out how important was the work and industry of that native population of which it is so hard to learn much from the direct evidence of the tombs. For the wall-paintings show us only the amusements of the wealthy and luxurious aristocracy ; it is very rarely that we can catch a glimpse of the strenuous life of merchant, artificer, or peasant. And there are no documents to inform us of their social and political relations. Only it may be inferred from the rigidity of the hierarchical system that the nobles of Lydian birth formed an absolutely exclusive and separate caste.

Games and amusements entered very largely into Etruscan life, and this is perfectly consistent with their Asiatic origin. The Lydians had tried, as Herodotus tells us, to forget the famine which at last drove them to emigrate, by abstaining from food on every alternate day and giving themselves up to diversion. It sounds like an ancient version of Boccaccio's *Decameron*, in which the gallants and the ladies fly from the raging plague to amuse themselves in the Villa Palmieri outside Florence. It was in this emergency, if we may believe Herodotus, that dice and ball-games, the pipes, and the trumpets, were invented. The Etruscans were certainly very fond of music, so that their wall-paintings show us the pipes, not the flute as is so often said, being played on every kind of occasion from a banquet to a funeral. Usually it is the

Phrygian double-pipe that is depicted, but in Plate
1, row 3 one of the musicians seated on the divan
is playing a syrinx with several tubes which looks
almost like a prototype of the organ attributed to
St. Cecilia by painters of the Renaissance. Opposite to him is a man playing the lyre. The Romans
borrowed much of this ceremonial; they also
had detachments of horse and foot-soldiers, pipe-
players and lyre-players in their processions. It is
known that the Roman pipe-players were quite
important people with a peculiar festival of their
own, and Livy tells us that on one disastrous occasion they all went on strike and ran away to Tivoli,
but were strategically made drunk and brought
home to their duties in a cart; after which they
were placated with fresh privileges. Wind-instru-
ments were especial favourites with the Etruscans,
who were credited with the invention of more than
one kind of horn or trumpet. The best known was
the lituus, which also passed into common use
amongst the Romans.

Of the character of the music it is impossible to
form any idea. Very often it was the accompani-
ment to a dance, but sometimes, as in the scenes
which we are studying, the players seem to be
executing a solo or a duet.

In the last two rows 5 and 6 of my Plate 1 is
shown the actual funeral *cortège* to which the other

scenes are an introduction and prelude. It centres upon the figures of two men clothed in long cloaks with broad-brimmed hats, who carry on a pole slung between them a bronze vessel of just the same form as the *situla* on which these reliefs are embossed. It is the cinerary urn containing the ashes of the dead person. This is rather an unexpected thing, because the normal Etruscan rite was not cremation but interment in the ground. The Etruscans certainly used both rites, but it has often been suggested that they themselves always buried their dead, and only borrowed the custom of cremation from the native Italians, who never did anything except burn. It is a disputed point and I think that it would be hard to prove that cremation is not a genuinely Etruscan habit. But it is open to any one who thinks the contrary to consider that this is the burial of a native Italian, who had risen to some prominence in the Etruscan colony of Felsina, the later Bologna, where this record was found.

In front of the cinerary urn three women carry respectively a bundle of faggots, a ribbed bronze vessel, and a basket. Next to them are three grave and reverend persons in long cloaks and large hats, while a splendid ox is led by a man in front.

Then behind the urn-bearers, row 5 shows in order a man leading a ram, three more reverend seigneurs, three women bearing bronze water vessels, a man with bronze bucket and pointed jar, and lastly a man with a bundle of skewers on his shoulder followed by a curly-tailed dog. In these two rows, then, we have the ox and the ram being led to the sacrifice, the servants carrying all the apparatus for the fire and offerings of food and drink, and half a dozen dignified relatives of the deceased marching gravely in their places.

The *situla* of the Certosa, on which are figured the little reliefs that have just been described, is a document of first-rate importance for the interpretation of Etruscan life. It was found at Bologna, and was for some years regarded as an importation from the Venetian city of Este, the centre of a separate and wholly un-Etruscan civilization. But the latest criticism has proved it to be genuinely Etruscan, and has shown that the Venetian examples are actually derived from it. The Certosa *situla* in fact became the prototype of quite a number of similar bronze-reliefs, which were exported out of the country and have been found as far afield as the Tyrol and Lower Austria. These imitations are all far inferior to the original, and the Alpine examples strike a note of grotesqueness and buffoonery quite unlike the spirit of the Bolognese artist. But the Benvenuti *situla* at Este is a very fine piece of work, less unlike the Certosa example in style, and very near to it in date. This *situla* gives some scenes not found in the Bologna reliefs —such as the inspection of a restive horse which the groom holds by one leg in front of its indolent master seated in a round-backed chair; not to speak of the almost inevitable boxing-match. In the Benvenuti specimen one zone represents a military triumph, the foot-soldiers are leading prisoners and are preceded by a chariot, while a trumpeter in one corner blows a curved horn.

I have said that the Certosa *situla* is to be dated about 500 B.C. This means that it belongs to a very advanced period of Etruscan art when the influence of classic Greece had come into full play ; indeed, the whole character and execution of the work shows that it is the product of a finished school with long traditions and a fully perfected style. Moreover, it came from an average commonplace grave, belonging evidently to a person of no special distinction. To us the accident of survival has made it a unique example, but to its contemporaries it would have seemed an ordinary standard piece of studio work, I might almost say of factory work. We must inquire, therefore, what were the beginnings and the origin of the school from which it emanated. Native Italian copper-smiths before the arrival of the Etruscan had no conception of artistic decoration. They had mas-

tered the difficult, though primitive, technique of
hammering out copper plates by hand, and rivet-
ing them together into forms of a certain grace and
dignity of outline.   But their knowledge of orna-
mental design went no farther than simple ar-
rangements of lines and angles ; they were at the
stage of art which is known as the ' geometric '.
Motives derived from flowers and vegetation, representations of animals and of men, were first
brought in from the East, inspired directly or in-
directly by the art of Egypt, Syria, and Mesopotamia.   It is a very striking circumstance that
motives of this kind appear, already in a fully perfected form, in almost the earliest Etruscan graves
discovered in Italy.   The famous ' Tomb of the
Prince ' at Vetulonia, which may be dated a little
before 700 B.C., contained a chest encased in
sheets of silver embossed with figures of men and
winged animals, birds, and leafy plants.   And in
the same tomb there was a silver cup ornamented
in low relief with human-headed sphinxes, bulls,
griffins, and rows of various birds.   These are the
products of a perfectly finished school of Oriental
art, worthy to stand beside the best work of Egypt
and the near East.   But we must not suppose that
they were made on Italian soil, it is obvious that
they were imported.

In the next generation the number of these imports from the East has enormously increased. A very brisk commerce was now going on between Etruria and the centres which produced these art objects in gold and silver. The copper of Tuscany and the iron of Elba were no doubt being shipped as raw materials in exchange. Accordingly, the great princely tombs of the early seventh century, which will be described in the next chapter, were full of the work of Oriental silversmiths and gold-smiths, as well as carved ivories decorated with the same motives. It is here then that we find an explanation of the wonderful mastery which the Etruscans had acquired by the fifth century. They had been practising and imitating foreign models for fully three hundred years. But a generation or two will be more than sufficient to produce a new native school; witness the American silver-work of the eighteenth century, or the Scottish develop-ment of French designs as they may be studied in the maces at St. Andrews.

In the great tombs of Caere and Praeneste, dated closely to about 670 B.C., were found silver-gilt bowls and dishes which clearly served as the origi-nal models for the Etruscan metal-workers of the next two hundred years. Precisely similar ex-amples have been unearthed on several sites in Cyprus, so that it is plain that they were manu-factured at some place in or near Syria. One of them is engraved with a Phoenician name, but it does not follow that it was of Phoenician workmanship ; I may write my name, I hope, in a French book in my library without any one suggesting that I am its author. So far the best archaeologists have been rather chary of suggesting the precise place of manufacture. But the near-Oriental school which produced this figured silver-work and the carved ivories which go with it was inspired from two very distinct sources, the one Egyptian and the other Assyrian. The inspiration may have been indirect, the artificers themselves were certainly neither Egyptian nor Assyrian, but they were working on a more or less stock *répertoire* of scenes and motives taken from life in those two countries. Sometimes the Egyptian note is entirely predominant ; thus in one bowl the sacred boat of Ra is shown at each corner, while the central medallion contains a figure of the Pharaoh triumphing over his enemies. On one ivory carving the horseman rides through thickets of papyrus, and another ivory is decorated with a lotus border of the purest Egyptian style. But in another example of this art the whole scenery and setting is Assyrian in character ; it is the story of a stag-hunt, in which the monarch issues from a Mesopotamian castle, and then dismounting pursues his game on foot, clothed in his long mantle and wearing a peaked cap. Entirely Assyrian also in feeling are the single-handed fights of men with lions and the combats of lions with bulls. Yet side by side with these are a few pieces in which the orientalism is far less accentuated and gentler scenes are depicted, with only figures of horses and cattle.

In Plate 2 I show two of these bowls, one from the Regolini-Galassi tomb at Caere and the other from the Bernardini tomb at Praeneste. On the Regolini-Galassi bowl the central medallion depicts two lions pulling down an ox, while the next zone is filled with a typically Asiatic hunting scene; a man engages a lion in single combat, footmen armed with bow and spear attack another animal that has felled one of their number, and a mounted man shoots his arrows in Parthian fashion while a stag bounds frightened off the hill.

Very similar stories are narrated on the Praeneste bowl, there is the same single-handed combat, the same pictures of a lion clawing a prostrate man, and lions fastening on an unfortunate ox, while the mounted archer shoots at them. But a part of the picture is filled with the peaceful life of the herdsman tending his cattle, the horses pasturing, and the workman trimming the tree under the direction of his master. It is this last part which has suggested the country scenes on the Certosa *situla,* whereas the Etruscan parade of foot-soldiers

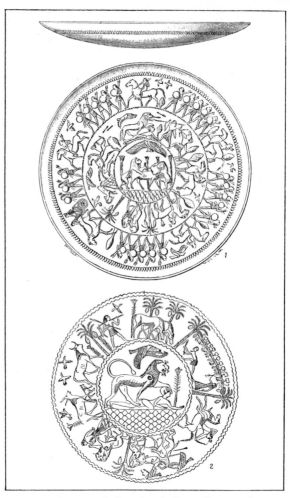

2. Engraved silver bowls from Caere and
Praeneste

is directly copied from the march of the army on the other bowl. Only the arms and equipment have been varied, so that instead of an Assyrian army with Oriental dress and weapons the Bolognese has shown the soldiers of his own time and country. Just in the same way a Renaissance painter would depict the characters of Bible history as garbed in the Florentine dress of his own day. By the fifth century the subjects which I have described had become the common stock-in-trade of every metal-worker; the technique and style had long been mastered, and figured bronzes of this kind must have been so frequent that more examples will probably be discovered in due time

The organization of society; A noble and his wife; Oligarchical government; Etruscan blood in Roman families; Life and manners of the aristocrats; Riches of nobles as shown by Regolini-Galassi tomb at Caere; Description of the tomb and its contents; Goldwork and jewellery; Similar tombs at Praeneste.

IN the last chapter we have had some glimpses of the ordinary everyday life of the common people, the native Italians who formed the working-classes and carried on the agriculture and industries on which the prosperity of the country was based. We know a great deal more of the nobility, whose richly furnished tombs have, indeed, supplied the principal evidence of Etruscan art and civilization. Between the two was a middle class of *bourgeoisie*, probably attached to the nobility by the bond of clientship in that technical sense in which the word ' clients ' is used by Latin writers. There was no bridge, however, by which any man of humbler birth could pass into the ranks of the aristocracy. Pride of race and descent was the very foundation of the conquerors' power, and the care with which genealogy is stated in the inscriptions shows that the Lydian nobles kept their escutcheons clean. The spindle-side was always remembered and respected; the mother's

3. A NOBLE AND HIS WIFE
Sarcophagus from Caere

family name is often carefully recorded. And throughout a very important position was always accorded to the woman, who is not only sculptured with her husband on the tomb but is shown beside him at the banquet and at public festivals and entertainments. This honoured position of the wife was a source of great astonishment to the Greeks, who were as incapable as any Mohammedan of appreciating it. Accordingly the Greek writers gave free rein to their malicious tongues, and invented a series of calumnies on the moral character of a people who, by the evidence of their monuments, are shown to have been far superior to the Greeks in all the essentials of a decent family life.

The appearance of an Etruscan noble and of his wife is familiar from several beautiful sarcophagi of terra-cotta obtained at Caere. One of these is in the British Museum, one in the Louvre, and a third in the Museo di Villa Giulia at Rome. From the last of these I have taken the illustration shown in Plate 3. The figures are half-sitting, half-reclining, on a bed which is a model of that which they had used in life, finely finished with decorated supports. The man is a grave and dignified personage, wearing long hair and a well-shaped beard but with the upper lip shaved clean. Under a close-fitting cap the wife has long plaited tresses hanging down upon her shoulders, a fashion that is repeated on almost every statue or representation of a lady of rank. She does not wear the jewellery and heavy ornaments which she usually wore in life, as we know from the frescoes no less than from the actual objects found in the tombs.

This group belongs to the end of the sixth or beginning of the fifth century, practically the same generation as the marvellous Apollo of Veii. It is perhaps affected somewhat by the Ionic-Greek style but is thoroughly characteristic of Etruscan statuary in its best period. It is interesting to contrast it with the much earlier stone head of a warrior from Orvieto in the museum at Florence. The Orvieto head is one of the earliest examples of Etruscan sculpture, usually dated to the seventh century.

At the beginning of their history, some, if not all, of the Etruscan cities were ruled by kings, if any confidence at all may be accorded to the numerous Latin statements. But the period of kingship was soon passed and the normal constitution was that of a very close oligarchy comparable with that of the Venetians in the great days of that Republic. A very small number of families ruled and governed each little state, maintaining all the privileges of a warrior caste, and with particular jealousy reserving all the functions of priesthood to them-

selves. Even in the days of Cicero the sole custo-
dians of the sacred lore were the nobles, and so
important was this knowledge to the Romans themselves that great Etruscan families must have been
very influential in Rome even down to the time of
the Empire. We know that Maecenas was proud
of his Etruscan blood. Propertius was of pure
Etruscan lineage ; while the very names of Sulla
and Catiline reveal their origin.

A common Roman name is *Lucius*, which is nothing but a Latinized form of the Etruscan *Lucumo*.
Varro glosses the word *Lucumones* as meaning
Etruscan nobles, and the word is often employed
by modern historians to denote the aristocracy in
general. It never appears as a simple name in any
of the inscriptions and is, therefore, probably the
title of official rank. It was the *Lucumones* who
transcribed the sacred books, and a Latin com-
mentator says that the twelve cities of the Confederacy were each headed by a *Lucumo*. That
priesthood was no bar to fighting efficiency is
shown by the story told of two battles against the
Romans, in each of which the Etruscan priests,
bearing torches in one hand and serpents in the
other, charged at the head of their forces and
struck terror into the ranks of the enemy.

When not engaged in the serious work of government, the interpretation of auspices or the service

of the gods, the nobility led a pleasure-loving and luxurious life, many sides of which are shown in the wall-paintings of the tombs. But in estimating the meaning of these scenes two things must be remembered. The first is that all the frescoes, especially from the fifth century onwards, are greatly influenced by Greek subjects and composition; the second is that they show only one side of Etruscan life, that is to say, the recreations, sports, and amusements that accompanied the banquet and the festival. The men who had become the scourge of the western seas, who had conquered half Italy and raised it from barbarism to a high civilization, did not spend their whole time in horse-racing, or in watching boxers and wrestlers to the sound of the pipes. English life is not completely represented by sporting prints, pictures of Derby Day, and the records of football or cricket matches.

The finest series of paintings are those of Corneto and Chiusi, and there will be more to say of them when I am speaking of these sites. Here it is more appropriate to convey some impression of the riches and luxury which are revealed by the excavation of three famous tombs, the contents of which are now in the great Museums of Rome. The period is the early seventh century, about 670 B.C., a hundred and fifty years after the conquest.

The Regolini-Galassi tomb derives its title from the names of the two speculators who entered into a partnership in 1836 to discover and exploit any buried treasures that might be found in the land of the arch-priest of Cervetri, as the ancient Caere is now called. They had the good fortune to find an untouched tomb built under a tumulus about half a mile from the modern town of Cervetri. Its general appearance is well described in the Victorian language of the admirable Dennis, who visited the site about ten years after the excavation.[1]

It must be remembered, however, that the date

' The sepulchre opens in a low bank in the middle of a field. The peculiarity of its construction is evident at a glance. It is a rude attempt at an arch formed by the convergence of horizontal strata hewn to a smooth surface and slightly curved so as to resemble a Gothic arch. This is not, however, carried up to a point but terminates in a square channel covered by large blocks of nenfro. The doorway is the index to the whole tomb, which is a mere passage about sixty feet long constructed on the same principle and lined with masonry. This passage is divided into two parts or chambers, communicating by a doorway of the same Gothic form with a truncated top. The similarity of the structure to the Cyclopean Gallery at Tiryns is striking ; the masonry it is true is far less massive but the style is identical, showing a rude attempt at an arch, the true principle of which had yet to be discovered.'

[1] Dennis, *Cities and Cemeteries*, chap. xxi.

of the Regolini-Galassi tomb is many centuries
after the Mycenaean, so that though the general
resemblance may be allowed for purposes of description, it must not be supposed that there is any
connexion between the two, except in so far as
they are equally the work of people whose architectural skill is very rudimentary. The origin and
connexions of Etruscan architecture constitute a
particularly difficult question which has never
been systematically studied, but it is interesting to
note from this tomb a point which is confirmed by
others of the same date, namely, that the principle
of the true arch was unknown as late as 670 B.C.

The tomb was divided into an antechamber and
a chamber, the former flanked by two oval re-
cesses. In the antechamber was buried a warrior,
laid on a bed of bronze which is perfectly preserved. In the chamber were all the ornaments
and jewellery of a woman whose body had fallen
into dust but whose bridal trousseau lay in place
precisely as she had worn it. The antechamber was
separated from the chamber by a low wall on which
stood the great bronze cauldrons. Along the roof
had been nailed bowls and dishes of silver and
bronze, and on the walls around the warrior had
been nailed bronze shields and bundles of arrows.
Near him stood a four-wheeled chariot, and in
the right-hand niche was a two-wheeled chariot.

Canina made a sketch of the position of the objects, which though not the work of an actual eye-witness is very valuable as it was based on information obtained on the spot. This sketch may be seen in either of his great folio volumes and has often been reproduced in books more easy of access.

The contents of this tomb were purchased *en bloc* by the Vatican and form the most important part of the Vatican Etruscan Museum. They have very recently been edited and rearranged, so that now, for the first time, they can be studied with ease and confidence. Good photographs of some of the finest objects may be obtained from Alinari.

If a few objects were undoubtedly imported, such as the silver-gilt bowls described in the last chapter, the bulk of the contents of the tomb must have been of local manufacture. This being so we should particularly notice the perfection of the bronze work. Unfortunately, the chariots had wholly perished, but the well-preserved cauldrons with lion-heads and griffin-heads are masterpieces. They resemble the cauldrons from Vetulonia of which examples are shown later in Plate 9 and the type was adopted for the great votive offerings sent to Olympia. Even more delicate and exquisite are a bronze censer on wheels ornamented with lotus-buds, and the bronze support of a cauldron on which griffins and animals are worked in low relief. Almost unique is the bed of cast bronze, strongly constructed with a framework of bronze bands; its headpiece is decorated with an Egyptian boat among palm-trees.

But it is the goldwork which will most impress the visitor to the Vatican Museum and the quantity and fineness of this is extraordinary. As the old accounts of it say, such a collection ' would not be found in the shop of a well-furnished goldsmith '. To give an idea of its character I have illustrated some of the pieces in Plates 4 and 5. Taking Plate 4 in the order of its arrangement No. 1 is a large fibula or safety-pin decorated with details in filigree and granulation. No. 2 *a*, of which 2 *b* shows an enlarged detail, is a chain of fine gold links terminating in lion-heads. No. 3 is a small gold plaque to be sewn on a dress; No. 4 is one of several pendants, stamped with a row of female figures and ornamented at the edges with granulations. No. 5 is another large safety-pin of gold; 6*a* is a silver jug with a honeysuckle motive, 6 *b*, at the base of the handle. Nos. 7–10 are silver cups, inscribed with the name of the owner *Larthia*.

In the next picture are shown two of the finest examples in the series. No. 1, of which a sectional view is given in 2, is an immense ornament in the form of a safety-pin. It is composed of two great discs of gold plated on a core of silver,

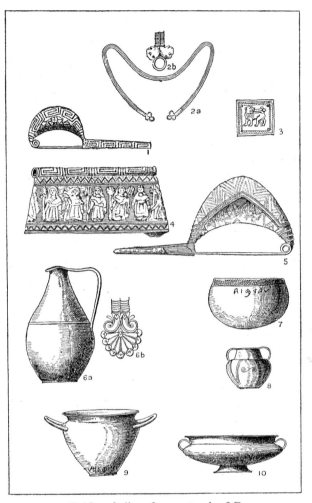

4. Gold and silver from a tomb of Caere

separated by two cross bars of finely granulated goldwork. On the larger of the two discs the central field is occupied by five lions in low relief, in the smaller there are seven rows of little ducks made in the round out of sheet gold and soldered on to the gold base, which is ornamented in the spaces between them with rows of winged lions in low relief. More beautiful though less remarkable as a mere *tour de force* is No. 3, a bracelet made of sheet gold with figures in relief and a border of granulated work. The top band shows a female figure standing upright between two conventiona-lized palm-trees. With each hand she holds one paw of a rampant lion whose other paw is laid upon her shoulder. Behind each lion stands a warrior armed with a sword which he is in the act of plunging into the body of the beast. Beneath this mythological representation is a row of three identical female figures precisely resembling the first but unaccompanied by animals. The reader who remembers my description of the silver bowl in the last chapter will at once realize that the scenes on this bracelet belong to the same school of Asiatic art. And to the same class belongs a gold pectoral, too large to be illustrated here, which is perhaps the most gorgeous surviving specimen of Etruscan goldwork. It is about eighteen inches high, made of thin sheet gold hammered round

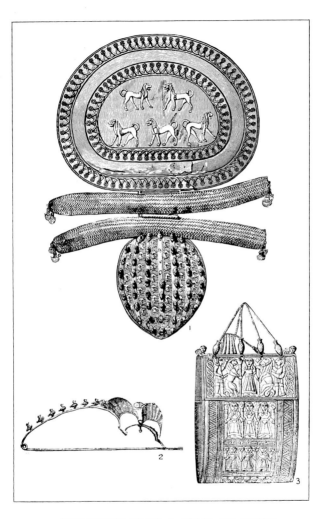

5. GOLDWORK FROM A TOMB AT CAERE

a core of copper which has perished. The heart of it is formed by an escutcheon made up of four rows of figures in relief. Round this are concentric zones of similar figures, twenty-one rows in all, the subjects being a man between two lions, then an entire row of lions, then a row of winged sphinxes.

It would need more space than can be given here to discuss this jewellery at length. Much of it is obviously inspired by foreign motives, and if not actually imported is at least imitated from that cycle of near-Asiatic art which I mentioned in the last chapter. But it may have been manufactured in Etruria and some pieces are certainly of native workmanship. For many years Vetulonia had been developing a school of very skilful goldsmiths, whose work as exhibited in the Florence Museum must be studied presently, and however much the Etruscans may have owed to foreign suggestions and influence it is probable that by this time they had their own goldsmiths and silversmiths.

Very similar in the general character of their contents, and evidently belonging to exactly the same generation as the Regolini-Galassi, were two tombs discovered at Praeneste, known in medieval and modern days as Palestrina. One point of great interest about these is that they are situated outside the borders of Etruria proper. This shows that Etruscan civilization had crossed the Tiber and penetrated into Latium as early as the beginning of the seventh century. A nobleman lived in exactly the same style about 670 B.C. whether his residence was in Caere or on the edge of the Sabine hills. Of the architecture of these two tombs nothing is known; the excavations were made in an unscientific period by people who aimed at making collections but not at increasing knowledge. The contents of one, called the *Bernardini* tomb and popularly described in the guide-books as the ' Treasure of Praeneste ', may be seen in the old Museo Preistorico at Rome—now renamed after its late director Pigorini. The other, known as the *Barberini* tomb, is in the Museo di Villa Giulia. The American Academy at Rome has recently published two admirably illustrated memoirs on the *Bernardini* and *Barberini* tombs, which bring the material within reach of every student.

The greater part of the bronze work at Praeneste is very similar to that of Caere; there are the same hand-hammered cauldrons of bronze on their iron stands, the same fluted bowls and general equipment of jugs and minor vessels together with one or two of more individual character. But the delicately carved ivories of the *Bernardini* and *Barberini* tombs add an important item to our knowledge of seventh-century art, and some of the goldwork is among the finest of its time. It is true that cumbrous great buckles, ornamented with rows of lions, sphinxes, and human-headed birds, are remarkable more as demonstrations of technical skill than as objects of beauty ; but the *Bernardini* gold skyphos, with two seated sphinxes on each handle, is a work of such exquisite taste that if it is not Greek I can only say that a Greek might have been very proud to have made it. Of a rare beauty also are some small gold clasps bearing winged sphinxes.

The beginning of the seventh century then is a time of the highest possible achievement in all the minor arts ; but architecture, sculpture, and painting are still in their infancy. For the preceding eighth century all that we know is to be learned from Vetulonia, which will presently be studied in a later chapter.

CHAPTER 4

NOT every site of a famous Etruscan city is to
be recommended for a visit. There are few
people who will not be disappointed with Chiusi,
an extremely dirty little town with a street of un-
mitigated ugliness ostentatiously named after Lars
Porsenna! A drive of some hours over the well-
tilled acres that cover the environs of ancient Clusium will betray the secret that most of the frescoed
tombs are now wrecked and ruined beyond all re-
cognition. The only one that has been saved from
destruction is the Tomb of the Monkey, which is
kept so carefully locked that it is very difficult to
find the keeper of the key. The local museum,
however, possesses a certain number of very fine
specimens which a specialist will find worth his
study, though he will be able to obtain no information as to their provenance or associations.

Vulci again, where the very important Polle-
drara tomb of the British Museum was found
many years ago, has been a place very rich in

tombs, the contents of which have been distributed far and wide. But it is extremely difficult of access and desolate beyond description. The hardy traveller who may find his way there will be rewarded with the view of some magnificent gallery tombs discovered since Dennis wrote, tunnelled in the side of the cliff facing the ancient city. For these, and for a topographical study of the place, an enthusiast may be willing to go there and will certainly not regret it. But the ordinary visitor to Italy will be better advised to read of Vulci as well as Chiusi in his Dennis, and to reserve his money and energy for places where there is more to see.

It is not difficult however, and it is well worth while for any one who may be staying in Rome, to make expeditions to Corneto (Tarquinia) and to Cervetri (Caere), two of the most ancient and important cities in Southern Etruria, which are extremely rich in objects of interest. Corneto is sixty miles from Rome on the direct line to Pisa. The picturesque medieval town is built on a high plateau, two miles above the railway station, at which, however, an auto-bus meets the train. There is an inn where it is possible to sleep, but which cannot be recommended to the luxurious. Without a full uninterrupted day, however, it is not possible to obtain more than a very slight idea of the tombs. So with this warning I will leave the reader to make his choice according to his philosophy of life. In the newly arranged museum housed in the fine Palazzo Municipale, a well-read student will be glad to pass at least some hours. The specimens are not arranged in tomb groups, for excavations in the old days at Corneto were not as scientific as they should have been. But the individual examples of pottery are unusually important, and this is the only place in which it is possible to study a class of geometric ware which is closely related to that of Cumae. One very important tomb group has been kept intact. It is from a grave which contained an Egyptian vase of blue faience embossed with a series of most unusual Egyptian scenes, and inscribed with the name of Bokenranf, the only king of the 24th dynasty, who is known to have reigned at Sais from 734 to 728 B.C. Genuinely Egyptian objects are extraordinarily rare so early as this in Italy, and a vase which is dated very closely by an inscription is absolutely unique.

To most visitors, however, the great interest of Tarquinia will be in its frescoed tombs. Many of these have been known for several generations, and the most famous have been picturesquely described by Dennis, whose accounts are of permanent value. Until recently no good copies of these

6. FRESCOES IN THE TOMB OF THE LEOPARDS AT CORNETO

paintings were generally accessible, but in the last few years much progress has been made towards publication. Weege's *Etruskische Malerei* is to be found in any good library; Poulsen's *Etruscan Tomb-paintings* is an inexpensive book which gives a good critical account of a selected series; and vol. vi of the *Memoirs* of the American Academy at Rome has some admirable reproductions in colour. Even those who are unable to visit Corneto for themselves may obtain a good idea of the paintings from these publications.

It is impossible in this little book to attempt any serious illustration of such a subject; but I have selected one example, a scene from the famous 'Tomb of the Leopards', as sufficiently characteristic to be worth description. On the pediment over the back wall are two hunting leopards, almost life-size. Beneath these a feast is in progress. The banquetters are reclining in pairs on three couches, of which only two appear in my illustration. On each of these may be seen a youth and a girl, the young men attired in mantles, the girls in chiton and mantle, all wearing garlands. They are served by naked boys, not naked women as the Greek writers falsely asserted to be the custom. On the side-wall is the usual pipe-player. The fresco dates from about 500 B.C., and the treatment, as Poulsen points out, is influenced by the style and composition of red-figured Attic vases, which were familiar objects at this time (Plate 6).

No wall-paintings indeed at Corneto are actually earlier than the sixth century; one of the earliest is the Tomb of the Bulls, which already represents a Greek story, Achilles watching for Troilus at the well, in a style quite perceptibly influenced by Ionic art. This detracts a good deal from their value as representations of Etruscan life; but when we have eliminated everything that is demonstrably Greek, there remain many details of custom, dress, and ceremony which are purely Etruscan. The most ancient of all the tomb pictures are those of the Grotta Campana at Veii, which are purely decorative in treatment and seem to be of the seventh century. Some of the latest are those in the ' Tomb of the Cardinal ' at Corneto, which belongs to the third century. There is a marked difference in the atmosphere of the several periods. The subjects in the later centuries are horrific scenes of escort to the underworld by terrible demons, anticipations of Orcagna's nightmares in the Campo Santo of Pisa. Those of the fifth and sixth centuries are laughter-loving revels as care-free as the tales of the *Decameron*. The main idea in these earlier frescoes seems to have been to depict the funeral banquet, with all the preparations and accompaniments of the funeral procession.

Probably the motive, just as in Egypt, was to ensure by magic a repetition in the underworld of the material pleasures which had been enjoyed in life.

Thus it is that the pictures illustrate, in a different medium and with far greater richness of detail, the same sort of theme that has already been observed in the bronze reliefs of the Certosa *situla*. But the subjects are chosen from the life of a luxurious capital, not from the sober existence of a countrified provincial town. The pleasures and amusements are those of the *jeunesse dorée*, not of the unsophisticated country bumpkins of the provinces. The practical side of a funeral feast is well seen in the Tomba Golini of Orvieto, which shows the preparation of food; meat, venison, and poultry hanging in the larder; cooks and bakers plying their tasks; all to the sound of the inevitable pipes. In the Tomb of the Inscriptions at Corneto is shown a part of the equestrian procession, and the frenzied dance from which the Salii derived their rites. The Tomb of the Chariots at Corneto, very Attic in composition, has a beautiful scene of dancing, above which are shown the preparations for a chariot-race. In the following pictures of the same tomb can be seen the grand stands with the spectators seated on them. In short it is an Etruscan Derby Day, in which the women, even the most staid matrons, are taking an immense interest.

Other frescoes, notably in the Tomb of the Augurs, show athletic contests, wrestling and prize-fighting.

Cervetri, the ancient Caere, can be reached by train but it is far preferable to take a motor from Rome. A moderately early start makes it possible to reach the town before midday. Thence it is a walk of two miles over the meadows, where no car or carriage can be taken, to the entrance of the excavations. These are enclosed by a wire fencing to keep out intruders, but once the names have been formally entered in the visitors' book everything is easy, and a very well-informed member of the staff, or perhaps the busy Director himself, is ready to conduct the visitor.

The necropolis of Caere is the most striking monument or series of monuments to be seen in all Etruria. Already in the days of Dennis most of the great tumuli had been opened, and the old traveller's account of them is quite worth reading. But the excavations recently made by Professor Mengarelli have entirely changed the whole aspect of this city of the dead, which now stands in its completeness as perfect as if it were a part of Pompeii. To call it a city is no exaggeration ; its extent was that of a large town, the rows of tombs are systematically divided by paved streets, while many of the tombs are planned like houses and decorated with all the details of domestic architec-

7. EXTERNAL VIEW OF THE GREAT TUMULI AT CAERE

ture. Of the ancient Caere itself nothing remains
except some traces of the town walls, skirting the
plateau in sight of which we walked to the necropolis. It was superbly situated and must have
been a majestic capital, containing a large population and ranking as one of the greatest cities of its
day. The Tyrrhene Sea is in full view only a few
miles away, so that on any sunny day the Caerites
could see their argosies returning home laden with
the merchandise of Greece. And when the war-
fleet sailed against the Phocaeans of Corsica they
may have watched it on its way for many hours.

The wealth and importance of any nobleman of
Caere may be inferred from the account that I
gave in the last chapter of the Regolini-Galassi
tomb. This was only one of scores of gallery tombs
concealed under the great tumuli which are
now open to view. Two of these huge circular
buildings flank the main path by which we enter
the necropolis; the photograph in Plate 7 shows
their external character. They are round drums
forty or fifty metres in diameter carved out of the
soft tufa rock, which was cut away so as to leave
them standing up from the level of the street.
Whether any courses of masonry should be added
to this foundation of natural rock depended on the
particular place. Sometimes the original cliff-face
was high enough to need no more additions. Often,

however, it was only a foot or two high and then the requisite number of courses was added in the form of oblong blocks. Sometimes, where the living rock scarcely rose above the level of the street pavement, it was necessary to make the round tambour entirely of masonry. On the basis of rock or masonry was piled earth at the angle of rest so as to make a conical mound.

Internally these larger tombs have galleries hewn out of the rock opening out into a series of large chambers a little below the street, from which they are entered by a sloping passage. These galleries are driven in from different points of the circumference, generally two or three to each tumulus. The several chambers inside vary considerably in dimensions and arrangement, but most of them are carved with architectural details in imitation of houses. The forms of the beams and rafters sculptured in the soft stone are clearly visible in the photograph of my Plate 8, which shows the interior of a tomb which is a veritable museum of contemporary life. On the walls are moulded in stucco all the weapons and armour then in use—swords, shields, greaves, helmets. And with them are the accessories of the kitchen, axes, spits, and meat dishes. The bugler too has his lituus or trumpet put up to commemorate him. Thirteen niches, two of which çan be seen in the picture, were hewn

out of the walls to receive the bodies of these warriors, each niche separated from the next by fluted
pilasters. There is a good account of this tomb in
Dennis, whose woodcut gives a clear idea of its
appearance. To Dennis I would also refer the
reader for an account of the ' Tomb of the Seats
and Shields ', of which the symmetrical scheme
precisely reproduces the ground plan of an ancient
house. Besides these the tombs called ' Dei Pilas-
tri ', ' Del Triclinio ', ' Dei Tarquinii ', and ' Dei
Sarcofagi ' are each interesting for one reason or
another. In the last mentioned three beautiful
sarcophagi of white marble have been left in place.

The tombs in the tumuli of Caere are of very
various dates. Great sepulchral monuments of
this kind once built were not lightly abandoned
but continued to be used for many generations. It
is not surprising, therefore, that some of the burials
are as late as the fourth century B.C. The majority
are far more ancient, but there is no proof that
even the oldest antedate the seventh century B.C.
This is in precise agreement with everything known
about tumuli in other parts of Etruria; the oldest
of them only begin just about 700 B.C. Before
this time the Etruscans apparently constructed
no monuments of architectural character; they
buried in plain trenches like those still used for
the humbler folk even in late days at Caere. Many

of these simple tombs may be seen on the right-hand side of the main street and in the more distant sections of the necropolis. Here sometimes on a day in early spring a fortunate visitor may see graves which are just being opened, and still have all their pottery and objects intact.

The very large collection of antiquities obtained at Caere will all be exhibited in due time in the Museo di Villa Giulia at Rome, but the process of building and equipping the new rooms there is so slow that at the moment of writing the museum is scarcely doing justice to the importance of the excavations. When the results are all shown, together with those from Veii which are also entirely unpublished, it will be possible to make a far more complete study of the minor arts, especially of the sixth and seventh centuries, than has ever yet been made.

The third site which should be visited from Rome is Veii, not because much remains to be seen there, but because the historical associations and romance of the place are so irresistible. It can be reached in a motor in about three-quarters of an hour from the city, but a bright sunny day is indispensable if the season be winter. Good walkers can take the train from Trastevere to La Storta, and make their way thence to Isola Farnese in about half an hour. From the medieval castle

8. INTERIOR OF THE TOMB OF THE STUCCOES AT CAERE

which stands between wild and steep ravines, a country lane leads down to the site of the ancient temple, of which only the foundations remain. It was in digging here that a fortunate excavator, working for the Government in 1916, found one of the finest extant works of Etruscan sculpture. This is the Apollo of Veii which forms the frontispiece of my volume.

The statue is of terra-cotta painted in polychrome, and to understand its attitude it must be realized that it formed part of a group of four figures. All the rest of the group is in dust or tiny fragments, except for an almost equally beautiful head identified as Hermes. From the fragments, however, it has been possible to recover the composition, which evidently represented Apollo, accompanied by a second person who is presumably Artemis, contending with Heracles over the body of a stag. This is a scene which, though it has no quite exact parallel, is closely analogous to the versions of Apollo myths given on Attic black-figured vascs, a fact which in itself rather suggests, though it does not necessarily prove, the date to be sixth century. But undoubtedly on other grounds of style and history it must be assigned to the sixth century, and perhaps to the last years of the century, say 520 or 510 B.C. It is nearly contemporary, therefore, with the pottery sarcophagi of Caere.

The impression which this statue makes in its shadowed room at the museum is so overwhelming that I hardly trust myself to describe it. Briefly I would say that this is the most perfect incarnation of an entirely remorseless inhuman god that can be imagined. The severity, the ruthlessness, the terrifying beauty haunt the memory. If this is Etruscan sculpture we know why the ancients admired it. And what volumes might be written on the contrast with an art like the Chinese!

The Apollo then is one of the masterpieces of that famous school of Veientine sculptors which is mentioned by Pliny. Vulca of Veii, he tells us on the authority of Varro, executed the statue of Jupiter for the Capitoline temple as well as a statue of Hercules for Rome. Plutarch says, moreover, that the chariot in terra-cotta which crowned the Capitoline temple was the work of Veientine artists. It is almost legitimate, therefore, to consider that in the Apollo we see an actual work from the hand of Vulca himself.

Of the temple behind which the Apollo group was discovered little now remains; the statues were not found in their original places, but had been covered up and buried outside the temple walls. We should like to fancy that some devoted priest thus saved them from the sack of the city by the soldiers of Camillus. But it seems from the description of the way in which they were lying that they had already been broken before they were buried. So that probably Giglioli, the author of the official account, is right in suggesting that they were found as fragments by the workmen who constructed a Roman road across the once sacred area of the temple and were deliberately re-interred from a sentiment of reverence or fear. We can understand that such gods as these were too dangerous to insult by ill usage.

The cemeteries of Veii extended for an immense distance round the town and even now have only been very partially explored. One large and important tomb, however, is all that remains open to view, the rest, both large and small, have all been filled up again. The one that can be seen is the well-known Grotta Campana about a mile away from the temple over the meadows. It is so familiar from the illustrations in many books that I need not describe it in detail. Poulsen considers that the primitive ornamentation is ' akin to that of Greek vase painting of the seventh century B.C. The pictures are purely decorative ; animals and fabulous animals such as lions, sphinx, deer, and panthers fill the surface side by side with lotus flowers and palmettos. There is no narrative element. . . . There is in these pictures neither any action nor any reference to death or the tomb.'

As the only representative of its period the Grotta Campana ought to be visited if possible.

Many a long day might be spent in wandering and dreaming about the site of Veii, but apart from the romance of the spot and its historic interest the student will learn more from the contents of the excavations shown in the Museo di Villa Giulia. I speak optimistically, in the hope that the alterations and changes in the museum will soon be completed, and that the official publication promised for more than ten years past may at length appear. The death of one of the principal persons engaged has naturally delayed the account; but it should be recognized as an absolute duty to the scientific world, as well as to the memory of Colini, that a full, careful, and detailed record should appear without more delay. The valuable exhibits which will be placed in the new galleries of the museum will lose half their meaning if there is no written description of their associations, and the type of tomb and place in which they were found. Veii has an especial importance for its peculiar local character, linking it on one hand with the Faliscans, and on the other with the earliest cemetery of Rome.

A beautiful and romantic drive may be taken from Rome to Città Castellana, which is the nearest point to the ruins of Narce and Falerii. And on the way may be seen the picturesque little towns of Nepi and Sutri which were the strategic gates of Central Etruria in early Roman days. From Narce and Falerii there are large collections of objects in the Villa Giulia, but I would only draw attention in this place to the architectural sculpture from the temples.

Several entire rooms in the museum are devoted to the terra-cotta adornments which once decorated the exterior walls of temples at Falerii, and at Satricum, a place in the Volscian hills about forty miles from Rome. An admirably written section in the official guide to the museum describes these and gives a short account of the general character of an Etruscan temple. It must not be supposed that we can know all about Etruscan temples from mere literary sources. Vitruvius, writing on architecture in the time of Augustus, has devoted to this subject a chapter which has been endlessly discussed and debated ever since the sixteenth century. Possibly he had under his eyes some restored and rebuilt sanctuary in Rome which enjoyed the reputation of high antiquity; but, as all the original buildings had disappeared centuries before Vitruvius composed his work, it is only as a result of excavations that we have been able to obtain any exact knowledge. At Falerii the remains of several temples were found of which considerable parts go back to the late sixth century and early fifth, though additions to them were made in the Hellenistic period. At Satricum the terra-cotta sculptures were principally of the sixth and fifth centuries, but a foundation deposit shows that a building stood on the same site as early as the seventh. There are also a few remains from temples at Alatri, Segni, and Nemi exhibited in the same rooms.

It was not until the fourth century that any temples were built of stone. Before this time the walls were always of unburned brick, the beams and roofing were of wood, and the supporting columns of bricks or wood. Only the foundations were of stone. It is the same type of building that we have seen represented by the roofs and pillars of the great tombs of Caere, where the wooden construction is counterfeited in the carved tufo. The cella was subdivided for every temple into three sanctuaries, dedicated to a triad of deities. In the Capitoline temple built by the Etruscans at Rome the triad consisted of Jupiter, Juno, and Minerva. When finished the wooden frame of the building was covered with painted and moulded reliefs in terra-cotta, which are represented by the cornices, antefixes, tiles, and acroteria now to be seen in the museum.

All these reliefs show a strong Greek influence

and could hardly be distinguished from Greek work of the same periods. As the general style seems to be precisely the same whether the temple was built in Etruria, Umbria, Latium, or Campania, it has been suggested that there were bands of travelling craftsmen who brought their services wherever they might be required. An analogy might be found in the history of Romanesque architecture, when the Comacine masters were executing their work all over Italy.

The best of the decorative terra-cottas in the sixth century are quite beautiful, but they are the work of journeymen and apprentices, not for a moment to be considered in the same category as the great Apollo. As we look on this masterpiece we can sympathize with old Cato, who preferred the ancient images of terra-cotta to all the new-fangled statues brought from Syracuse and Athens, and may echo the words of Juvenal ' fictilis et nullo violatus Iupiter auro '.

THE most important sites in Central and Northern Etruria are less accessible than those of
the south. Orvieto, however, and Perugia are on the
regular tourist track. The rows of masonry chambers at the foot of Orvieto—which may have been
the original Volsinii—are still worth seeing, though
less attractive than they were twenty or thirty
years ago when so much of the pottery and other
objects remained in place. At Perugia the remains
of the walls and the Romano-Etruscan gates are
very striking ; and the third-century tomb of the
Volumnii is one of the finest examples of its period,
while the tomb of S. Manno also deserves a visit.

Cortona can be seen by stopping off between
two trains on the line from Florence to Perugia.
All who really care for Italian painting will make
an effort to go there for its Signorelli pictures, and
must spare just half an hour for the museum in
order to see a unique piece of Etruscan bronze
work, the famous candelabrum. The centre of
this is formed by a Gorgon's head, round which are

wild beasts, satyrs, sirens, and heads of Bacchus, of marvellous workmanship. The famous tumulus of Camuscia is in the neighbourhood, but the little that was ever found in it has gone to Florence.

Arezzo, dear to all lovers of Piero della Francesca, is kind enough to possess a passably good hotel; but the museum, though very interesting for its Roman objects, is not important for our purposes. Arezzo in fact is of relatively late foundation as an Etruscan city, though it was the birthplace of the bronze Chimaera, discovered in the sixteenth century and now in the Florence Museum.

None of these places, however, can compare in importance to any of those in a chain of sites extending along the Tuscan Maremma from Corneto to the headland of Piombino. The train *de luxe* from Paris passes through all this country, which the guide-books have conspired to call uninteresting. Few of the tourists bound for Rome trouble to look long out of the window—a novel seems more attractive. Hardly a foreign traveller ever passes this way except in an express train; there are no hotels to speak of and very few towns of any size. But for an archaeologist who knows his subject every mile is full of history, and nothing can be more fascinating for those who have any sense of the romance of the past than a motor-drive along this quiet coast. Quitting Civitavecchia to travel

northwards we leave on our right the mountains
of Tolfa and Allumiere, where graves have been
found of the old people who lived there as far back
as 1100 or 1200 B.C. Inland, north-east of Corneto,
are Norchia and Castel d'Asso, more easily visited
from Viterbo ; they are interesting for their rock-
tombs with architectural façades described by all
the old writers. At Montalto is the side-road to
desolate Vulci, but unless you have long hours to
spare you will leave it for another day and push on
to Orbetello, charmingly situated on the sea at the
foot of Monte Argentario.

On a hill to the left just before Orbetello is Anse-
donia, the ancient Cosa, an Etruscan site afterwards settled by the Romans. Its walls and towers
are marvellously preserved, but with all respect to
Dennis I feel some doubt whether they can be
called Etruscan rather than Roman. But the
activity of the Etruscans in this region is demon-
strated by one of their remarkable engineering
works, the emissary of the Lake of Burano.

The coast all along this region has greatly
changed since the earliest Etruscan days. Argentario in the ninth century B.C. may have been still
an island, and Vetulonia certainly rose straight up
from the sea instead of being cut off by miles of salt
marshes. Little rivers like the Albegna, Osa, and
Ombrone, which we hardly notice in passing, have

brought down masses of silt and must have added considerably to the acres of those who care to till. On the Albegna was Marsiliana, a seventh-century Etruscan settlement, which has yielded much to enrich the Florence Museum. A little farther on is Talamone, the ancient Telamon, a flourishing port of later foundation, famous in the third century as the scene of a great battle between Gauls and Romans.

At Grosseto we may pass the night at an inn which is technically described as ' discreto ' and needs no stronger adjective either of praise or blame. The next day, having assured ourselves that the engine is strong enough for the very severe climb, we may ascend the mountain of Vetulonia, which will take about an hour and a half from Grosseto. Unfortunately, there is no one alive in Vetulonia whose memory goes back to the time of the principal excavations. The priest is a well-informed man who can point out the places of some of the most important graves, but it is not easy to make such a detailed topographical study as one would wish. Little now remains above ground, and the only structure which can be studied is the tholos tomb of La Pietrera, somewhat too much restored, but carefully preserved as a national monument. Nevertheless, any one who wishes to understand Vetulonia should see the place, and I should particularly like to show it to a reviewer who reproached me with not making a wholly new map of it. After walking over the sides of the steep mountain, furrowed in every direction with steep ravines, he would understand that a single individual could hardly hope to make an adequate survey. But it is to be hoped that the Government, which can command the necessary men and resources, may some day furnish the world with a better archaeological map than has hitherto been available. For Vetulonia is a site of unequalled importance. Here was one of the earliest settlements, if not the very earliest, that was made by the Etruscans on their landing, and we are able to trace their graves from almost the first generation. Previously, this superb position had been occupied for many generations by the native Italians. Their cemeteries occupy a well-defined area, at the edge of which there appear new types of graves, with new rites and many imported objects clearly testifying to the presence of the foreign invaders.[1]

The most characteristic and important graves at

[1] For those who are sufficiently interested to study Vetulonia in detail I may perhaps say that there is a long description of it, with illustrations of the most important objects, in my *Villanovans and Early Etruscans*, published by the Clarendon Press in 1924.

Vetulonia were either tumuli or else circles of a kind to which there is no precise analogy elsewhere. These averaged 15–20 metres in diameter, and were outlined by slabs planted vertically in the ground edge to edge. Within the ring so formed were one or more oblong trenches containing the burials, which were more often of the inhumation than the cremation rite. Names have been given to the principal circles suggested by the character or by the most striking objects found in them ; and it is by these names that they may be recognized in the Florence Museum, to which I must now conduct a presumably not too unwilling reader.

On the ground floor of the museum is the series of rooms called ' Museo topografico dell' Etruria ', the first four of which are devoted to ' Vetuloni-enses '. Passing through a room given up to the predecessors of the Etruscans we come to a glass case labelled ' Tomba del Duce ', which contains the silver-covered chest in which the ashes of the great man were laid. It is ornamented in repoussé with figures of mythical animals, in the same style as the gilded-silver cup which may be seen in a case near it. Close by is a great bronze basin, made in a single piece without joints, originally covered with a circular shield under which in a confused mass were bronze bowls and candelabra.

They still lie exactly as they were found by Falchi, the explorer to whose devotion we owe almost the whole of the Vetulonian collection. On the top of the shield was the warrior's helmet. In another trench within the same circle was a second bronze basin of the same kind, filled with a remarkable variety of objects ranging from buckets to candelabra. Still another deposit contained the chariot, of which little remained except the iron wheels. Among the pottery, which includes some fine specimens of early bucchero, is a handled cup with an inscription of forty-six letters in the Etruscan alphabet, which is one of the earliest examples of its use.

The 'Tomba del Duce' or 'Tomb of the Prince'—to give it a convenient English equivalent—is the best known of the Vetulonian tombs, and has been much discussed and compared with the Regolini-Galassi and Praeneste tombs described in Chapter 3. It has many points of similarity in its contents, but I consider it to be a generation or two earlier.

Other tombs which have points of analogy with the 'Tomba del Duce' and the 'Regolini-Galassi' are the 'Circles of Le Pelliccie' and the 'Circle of the Cauldrons'. The first circle of 'Le Pelliccie' contained fragments of the chariot which was always placed in any large grave on this site, with the iron bits of the horses, a pair of bronze greaves, a bronze helmet, an axe, the butt of a spear, some important bronze vessels and fibulae of bronze, silver, and gold. The Second Circle of ' Le Pelliccie ' had the usual remains of a chariot, some fine bronze vessels, an iron spear, bronze spears, and a number of personal ornaments in gold, silver, amber, and glass. The gold and silver jewellery in these two graves is of exceedingly fine workmanship; the fibulae are mostly executed in the granulated technique but one has lines of filigree. The ' Circle of the Cauldrons ' is so called from the two splendid bronze vessels of hammered bronze, one decorated with the heads of lions and the other with the heads of griffins, which are shown in my Plate 9. Between the heads are very remarkable figures ; in the lion bowl it is a man with the wings and tail of a bird, in the griffin bowl it is a Janus-headed man with a bearded face like an Assyrian, wearing on his head a curious recurved cap.

From Vetulonia the Romans considered that they derived the insignia of their magistrates, the curule chair and the fasces, the purple toga and the trumpets. It was, therefore, particularly appropriate that in one tomb there should be found an actual specimen of the ' fasces et securis '. The axe is of iron double-headed, hafted on to an iron rod surrounded by eight hollow rods of iron. The happy discoverer named this the 'Tomb of the Lictor' and appropriately quoted the lines of Silius Italicus:

> Maeoniaeque decus quondam Vetulonia gentis
> Bissenos haec prima dedit praecedere fasces;
> et iuxit totidem tacito terrore secures.

In addition to this unique specimen the 'Tomb of the Lictor' contains some exquisite gold jewellery which will be described later.

In Plate 10 is shown a photograph which may give the reader some idea of the richness of these tombs which I must describe so summarily. From the great implement which stretches all across the picture it is called the 'Circle of the Trident'. Actually, however, the implement has nothing to do with the sea-god; it was probably used on land in the process of winnowing grain. The bronze discs, rings, and pendants, which occupy so much room in the illustration, are all parts of the equipment and harness of the horses. There are thirty-nine very large bronze safety-pins, and ninety armlets of various designs; sixteen bronze vases, and the remains of bronze pails, as well as spits, candelabra, and axes. What strikes us so particularly in a tomb-set like this is the enormous quantity of metal and the prodigal use that was made of it. This must mean that the copper mines of Tuscany

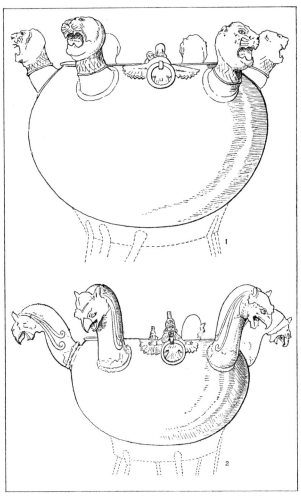

9. Cauldrons of hammered bronze from Vetulonia

were being exploited with immense energy, and that the whole country was full of bronze foundries. The old process of hand-hammering is still in use, but casting has also become very common. It is an extraordinary development of industry as compared with anything that could be seen a century earlier in the same district. And the free use of iron, employed regularly for the chariot wheels, proves that the commerce with Elba was very active. Silver and gold were also in common use ; several of the large tombs contain jugs or bowls of silver, and necklaces, clasps, and fibulae of silver are quite common. Gold, however, was the principal metal used for jewellery, and the abundance of gold in the Vetulonian tombs is quite striking.

The work of the goldsmiths of Vetulonia must have been famous all over the country. Examples of it are found even north of the Apennines, showing the existence of trade with the Bolognese several generations before any colonization had begun in that region. Almost every tomb has some beautiful piece in it, and there is a steady progress in the technical skill displayed. The earliest technique is of two kinds, either filigree work of fine wires twisted in maeanders separated by flat bands, as may be seen in the bracelet No. 3 of Plate 12, or else a granulating process which makes patterns by a combination of little pinheads.

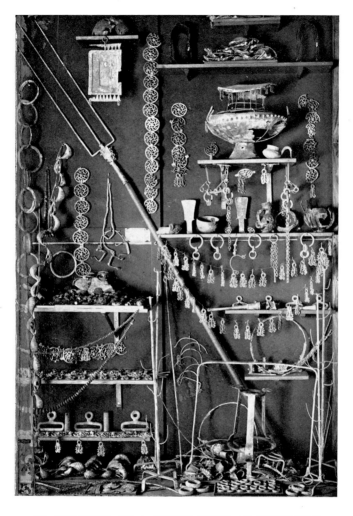

10. CONTENTS OF A CIRCLE TOMB AT VETULONIA

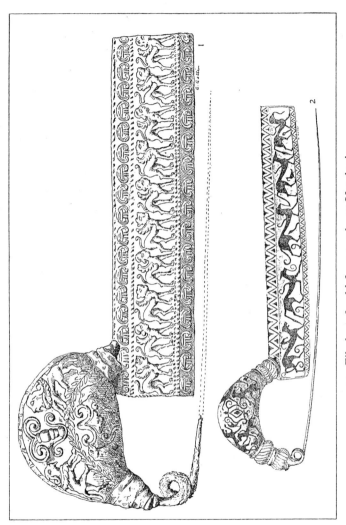

11. Fibulae of gold from tombs at Vetulonia

Granulation is well exemplified in No. 2 of Plate 11. It is a process of extraordinary difficulty which modern goldsmiths find quite hard to reproduce, and it was used with the most remarkable skill. There was a little work of this kind in the Regolini-Galassi tomb of Caere, but there it was already beginning to pass out of fashion, being superseded by repoussé. Here at Vetulonia we find the earlier stages, and can trace the gradual evolution by which a process very well adapted for the geometrical style of art has to give way to the technique of hammer and punch as soon as elaborate figures are required. The high-water mark of the granulated decoration is reached in such examples as No. 1 in Plate 12. Repoussé combined with filigree is seen in the very fine bracelet No. 2 of Plate 12, which may be contrasted with No. 1 of Plate 11, a piece of factory work in which ribbons of gold had been stamped by the yard and then very carelessly cut into lengths.

Gold jewellery was found in many graves, there were a score or so of the simpler filigree bracelets; but the finest and most artistic pieces of all kinds are those from the Lictor's tomb, and Le Migliarine, and from the small graves in the outer part of the tumulus of La Pietrera. There is reason to suppose that these are some of the latest of the Vetulonia series, and I think that they should be

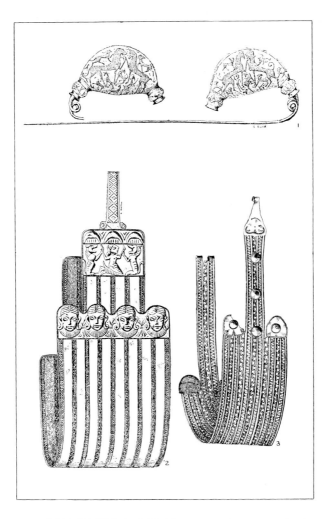

12. GOLD FIBULA AND BRACELETS FROM VETULONIA

dated just about 700 B.C. or a few years later, little earlier than the time of the Regolini-Galassi group. But the simpler bracelets and fibulae of more naïve workmanship seem to be several generations earlier and probably the full education of the artificers of Vetulonia occupied about a hundred years.

I am almost alone in maintaining that the Vetulonian graves are to be spaced over the whole century from 800 to 700 B.C., the majority of archaeologists bringing them all down to the later date. But there are very good reasons for my contention, and I have never considered it to be more scientific to understate a date than to overstate it. There is a curious prejudice in the human mind whether in golf or in archaeology. It is apparently quite orthodox to be six feet short with a putt but quite criminal to be six feet past the hole. And yet the distance to the hole is the same from either side !

In a room adjoining are the antiquities obtained from Marsiliana, situated on the little river Albegna a few miles south of the great mountain of Vetulonia. Marsiliana was admirably situated for trade ; it was virtually on the sea-coast, but the small rivers running down from the hills furnished a series of natural roads to the inland towns round the lake of Bolsena. The settlement is contemporary with the later part of Vetulonia, and we might almost guess that the town on the Albegna was actually a Vetulonian colony; its date, therefore, is early seventh century. In most respects the arts and crafts of Marsiliana are very similar to those which have just been considered in the preceding rooms, and there is no strong note of local variation. Jewellery and articles of adornment are in the main the same that were noted at Vetulonia, though Marsiliana adds a few types which show connexion with Southern Etruria. The extraordinary abundance of iron is particularly striking, and it is remarkably well preserved. There are not only weapons and chariot wheels but actually an iron bed quite complete. But the most interesting and novel objects at Marsiliana are the carved ivories, which must be compared and contrasted with those from Caere and Praeneste mentioned in my account of the Regolini-Galassi group.

An ivory comb is an exceptionally fine example. It is decorated with figures of animals. On the top are two feline creatures carved in the round, one on either side of an open pomegranate flower. Beneath these the body of the comb has a pair of winged sphinxes on the obverse and a pair of heraldic lions on the reverse, all carved in low relief. At each end of the comb are two volutes ending in griffin-heads.

A cylindrical ivory box, of the type called a 'pyxis', has a lid ornamented with a beautifully carved lotus flower, round which are represented in graffito various animals standing over a prostrate man armed with an axe. A somewhat analogous scene is represented in low relief on the two zones of the box itself; in the upper zone a prostrate man is attempting to defend himself with a knife against two lions, while two horned creatures fight one another and birds of prey hover over them; in the lower zone men are being devoured by lions, while a ram and a sphinx stand by in contemplation.

A less highly decorated ivory from the same tomb is of unique interest for another reason than its art. It is a writing tablet about three and a half inches long, on the edge of which a series of twenty-six letters is incised in strong clear lines running from right to left. This is one of the earliest examples of the Etruscan alphabet. It would be very interesting to know whether it was a present sent over to this wealthy family by a friend on the coasts of Asia Minor, or whether it was carved by some lover of learning in the Tuscan Maremma. All the ivory carvings in these tombs are inspired by foreign influence; they belong to the same school as those of Caere and Praeneste and are of almost exactly the same date.

Large fragments of chariots were found in the circle graves of Marsiliana, amongst which were two bronze triangular plaques decorated in relief with the figure of a warrior. These were very probably the frontal pieces of armour worn by the horses.

But the most perfect example of a chariot which has so far been noted came from Populonia and may be seen in the next room. Populonia is situated in a little bay north of the headland of Piombino. It is within easy reach of a motor-drive from Grosseto, and though there are only a few tombs to be seen they are distinctly interesting. Discovery proceeds by steady but slow stages, as the cemetery has been entirely covered up by the scoriae for the smelting furnaces. This refuse, however, repays reworking in modern times, and, as it is gradually removed by the company which has leased the site, the old tombs of the sixth century are brought to light in a state of very fair preservation. They are chambers each surrounded by a circular tumulus built of stone blocks. Populonia owed its importance and prosperity, as I have already said, to its neighbourhood to Elba, which is less than six miles from the point of Piombino, so that for practical purposes it belongs to the mainland. In ancient days, however, it was always found convenient to carry the ore over to Populonia, where presumably fuel was more abundant. Here it was smelted and traded all over Italy. In due time this site may be able to give a most valuable and complete record of continuous history, but so far the results have naturally been somewhat episodical. The chariot is a fine piece of early work, though it is, of course, far from complete in its preservation. It is an extraordinary fatality that has destroyed so many hundreds of the chariots which were buried in Etruscan graves. Only one first-class specimen exists, namely, the wonderful chariot from Monteleone near Spoleto, now in the museum at New York. This is decorated with superb reliefs in Ionic style, which are, however, so thoroughly Greek in their feeling that they are hardly representative of Etruria proper.

A fourth-century tomb at Populonia has yielded two painted Attic vases, and some fine bronze vessels. A set of gold jewellery from this site is generally supposed to have come from the same tomb, but there is no positive evidence on the point. Most of it may belong to that date, but a bracelet of fine filigree work is much more in the Vetulonian style and unquestionably earlier. Accessories are constantly being made to the Populonia room which will repay study.

Before passing on to other rooms in the ' Museo topografico ' the reader should visit the garden, which is an outdoor museum of the most attractive kind where models of characteristic tombs are shown built up on the original scale and sometimes with the original material. Here he may study the early vaulting of the tholos type as shown in a tumulus at Vetulonia, and a no less ancient ' cupola tomb ' from Casal Marittima. Here too he may see typical masonry chambers from the cemetery of Orvieto and numerous stelae from the same site, as well as graves from other places in some of which the pottery and accompanying objects are left in their original places. In their setting of flowering trees and orange bushes these make an Italian garden of unique charm, which may even persuade some people that archaeology is not incompatible with a certain sense of beauty, doubtless rudimentary but still capable of cultivation.

CHAPTER 6

Volterra and its antiquities ; The character and interest of the site ; Return to the museum of Florence and description of its important antiquities from Chiusi ; The pre-Etruscans of Tarquinia ; Bucchero pottery ; Carved sarcophagi and models of houses ; Masterpieces of bronze sculpture in the museum of Florence, especially the Chimaera and the Orator.

IF I devote another short chapter to the Museum at Florence it is because that is the only place in the world where Etruscan art and antiquities can be studied at all comprehensively as a whole. Almost every large museum in Europe has some Etruscan specimens of one kind or another, often remarkably fine ; but they are isolated and divided from all their proper surroundings, generally made to serve as a pendant to the Greek or the Roman, and hardly ever properly appreciated. In Italy itself there is only one other collection of any considerable range or importance, namely, the Museo di Villa Giulia, and that is confined to Southern Etruria. But in Florence the whole history can be studied from first to last, and owing to the excellent arrangement of the subject all the regional differences and peculiarities can be observed.

In the room which opens out into the corridor leading to the garden we see the battered effigy of

Larthi Atharnies. It was found near Volterra, which gives me an opportunity to speak of that strange grim place, otherwise not mentioned in this volume for a curious reason now to be explained. Of ' lordly Volterra ' hardly any traces remain earlier than the last century or two of the Roman republic. This is due to the destruction caused by the great landslips. Where the more ancient Etruscan cemeteries once stood are now yawning gulfs ; the graves have been plunged into the abyss. A few fragments of information have been rescued almost by accident. Thus on the site known as La Guerruccia a landslip thirty-five years ago revealed a series of graves, of which several are important as dating from the exact stage at which the earliest Etruscan influences appear. Some of the objects are in Florence, others at Volterra itself. With the few distinctly Etruscan graves were others of the native Italians. This small find is extremely valuable as confirming what we should otherwise have only known from the warrior's gravestone, namely, that there was really an Etruscan settlement at this remote spot as early as the first days of Vetulonia. But from the seventh century to the full Roman period there is otherwise no trace of any antiquities.

Dionysius counts Volaterrae among the cities which aided the Latins against Tarquinius Priscus;

but there is no other literary record of the place until 298 B.C. when L. Cornelius Scipio fought a fierce battle beneath its walls. But Dennis is no doubt right in saying that Volaterrae commanded a large territory, controlling the seaports of Populonia and Luna. Until recently it has been singularly inaccessible to the modern traveller. To go there by rail via Cecina is an exceedingly tedious expedition, which after making it myself I can hardly recommend. The only really practical method is to motor from Florence ; a public autobus makes the journey at extremely inconvenient hours, but with a private car it is quite easy. Certainly no traveller with an eye for the picturesque and dramatic should fail to see Volterra whatever trouble it may entail. It is one of the most majestic and awe-inspiring sites in Italy. Perched on its precipitous mountain nearly two thousand feet above the sea the city is still surrounded with very fine walls, admirably described by Dennis. In the museum which is not otherwise important is an extraordinary collection of carved sarcophagi made of the alabaster which is the local material. There are, I believe, no less than 600, ugly and gaudy rococo works of the third and second centuries B.C., principally representing Greek mythological scenes, but occasionally adding a detail of the local life which is not without value. ' Guarda e passa ', however, is generally the watchword of those who see them, and I do not advise to the contrary.

Returning to the Florence Museum we may glance at the few specimens which I have mentioned from La Guerruccia, and then pass on to an extremely important room devoted to the neighbourhood of the ancient Clusium. There are few good museums in Europe which do not possess at least a few specimens from Chiusi. That unfortunate region, which must be taken to include a considerable area round the modern town, was ruthlessly exploited all through the nineteenth century and its antiquities have been scattered far and wide. The only important public collection in Italy outside Florence is by a curious accident at Palermo, where it is neither appreciated nor studied; and it is much to be wished that it could be restored to Tuscany, as it contains material which is very important for the history of sculpture and bas-relief. It is solely due to the scientific spirit of Milani, the late director of the Florence Museum, that in this one place it is possible to study Chiusan antiquities as a whole. And this is very important because they have a strongly marked local individuality.

The peculiarity of Chiusi is that it always practised cremation, a rite which is otherwise sporadic rather than customary among the Etruscans. I

attribute this to a long persistence and survival of
the old Italian habits. There were Villanovan
settlements at Camars—to use its ancient name—
centuries before the Etruscans arrived there, and
we may even doubt whether the latter people settled in this region at all early in their history. Certainly the people of Clusium were not at all Etrus-
canized until the middle of the seventh century,
and the local habits survived for many generations
after that. This may be explained by the geo-
graphical position, which is far inland away from
the sea. But Lars Porsenna begins to appear as
something of a parvenu. His family was probably
much less distinguished than that of the proud
Tarchons of Corneto, who really did come in with
the Conquest. Was Porsenna after all only climb-
ing into society when he roused the clans against
Rome?

It is certainly an archaeological fact of a good
deal of importance that in its customs and culture
Chiusi differs from Tarquinia more than the semi-
Latin communities of Falerii and Narce. The
habit of incineration developed a peculiar form of
art which in its beginnings at least is rather local
Villanovan than true Etruscan. First of all
bronze or pottery masks were attached to the
cinerary urn, and from this stage the Clusians
passed to moulding the bust and arms in pottery

with a curious *naïveté*. This is the explanation of
an extraordinary series of grotesque jars, in-
accurately called ' Canopics ' from the mistaken
idea that the custom was analogous to the Egyptians, whereas it is precisely the reverse. The
Chiusan jars of course contained not the viscera
left over from embalmment but the ashes of the
dead. Of these so-called ' Canopics ' a number
may be seen in Florence, and there are one or two
in most foreign collections. They have a wide
range of date, beginning as early as 800 B.C. and
continuing till 600 B.C. Though the earlier examples are very crude some of the heads in the
succeeding century are remarkably well modelled,
and it is quite likely that this long schooling produced expert sculptors at Chiusi. A bronze ossuary
with a pottery head placed on a fan-shaped chair
ornamented with Etruscan winged horses is the
finest example yet known. But all, even the most
primitive, have useful lessons to teach in regard to
dress and ornament.

From the anthropomorphic pottery jar it was a
natural progress to the statue. A fine example of
a full-sized pottery statue, made hollow so as to
receive the ashes, is as late as the fifth century, to
judge from the Attic oenochoe found inside it.
Far earlier, unless they are deliberately archaizing,
are the statue of a woman with long tresses hang-

ing down on her shoulders, and the goddess who surmounts the Primoli ossuary. This remarkable piece belongs probably to the seventh century; the body of the ossuary is decorated in very low relief with a band of twenty identical figures in shapeless robes. Above these at four equidistant points are four human masks, which are matched on the lid by four large heads of long-necked geese, between each of which stand three little birds. The goddess is clothed in a long robe, the back of which is ornamented with stars; on her arms she wears armlets, and round her neck is a necklace of discshaped pieces joined by a scarab in the centre.

It is only towards the middle of the seventh century that Etruscan work at Chiusi begins to be artistically attractive. A very notable tomb-group of this precise date is furnished by the contents of a grave at Poggio alla Sala. On a bronze chair, differently shaped from the fan-backed fauteuils which are so familiar at Caere and elsewhere, stands a simple bronze urn which once contained the ashes. Traces of the cloth, perhaps originally purple, which covered the urn can still be detected. In front of the chair is a simple bronze table, below which are a bronze basin and platter, a large two-handled jar of pottery, a pottery jug, and several small vases for unguents. On the table may be seen some more little vases of early Greek fabric. The smaller vases are proto-Corinthian imported ware, the larger pieces may be of local manufacture but are influenced by Greek models. It is a curious symbolism that we see here, by which the burial-urn is treated as though it were a person, and placed in the dead man's seat in front of his table as if at a banquet. Swords and shields were found in this grave; the linen cloth over the ossuary was partly covered with gold leaf, and on the chair were some small ornaments and two bone dice.

From the Pania tomb of the same date may be seen a magnificent ivory *situla* about 11 inches high, carved with scenes of men and animals in four rows, separated by narrow bands of honeysuckle pattern, with a running border of lotuses above and below. The top row has a unique representation of a boat, preceded and followed by men and animals. Below this is a chariot followed by men on horseback and on foot, reminding us of the processions in the silver bowls of Caere and Praeneste and forming a definite link with the art of Southern Etruria. It should be compared with a silver bucket from Chiusi, exhibited on the upper floor, which is signed with the name Plicasnas, and beautifully engraved with a line of foot-soldiers round the middle and a row of animals at the base. Some details are known

as to the objects which accompanied the ivory
situla of this Pania tomb. It had been plundered in
ancient days, so that the floor was found strewn
with fragments of blue, green, and yellow glass.
There had been two burials, one of a skeleton and
the other of a cremated body, the ashes of which
were enclosed in a bronze ossuary not unlike the
one at Poggio alla Sala but with a larger neck.
Outside the bronze *situla* containing the ossuary
lay an exquisite gold fibula decorated with granulation, which is now at Berlin. There were iron
spear-heads and axes, a bronze chair, and fragments of many bucchero vessels, one of which had
been a large basin surrounded by griffin heads in
the style of the bronze cauldrons of Vetulonia. A
second ivory *situla* from another tomb at Pania is
of slightly later date, to judge from the carvings,
which represent the Greek story of Geryon, the
Cyclops, and Odysseus; its pottery, however,
assigns it still to the seventh century.

Before leaving the Chiusi room we should notice
a polychrome sarcophagus of alabaster from Città
della Picve showing a man and his wife. The
woman is wearing the actual gold necklace found
in the tomb with her, which seems to be a correct
interpretation of the fact that her neck was bored
with holes for such an ornament. This is dated
about 400 B.C.

The room entitled 'Tarquinienses' will be something of a surprise to any one who is thinking of the advanced art of Corneto as it is seen in the tombs. But the contents of this room are several centuries earlier; in fact they do not belong to the Etruscans at all but to their predecessors. Hitherto I have spoken of those predecessors by the general term of 'Italians', but now that we see their products I shall give them a more technical name and call them the 'Villanovans of Etruria'. This is in order to make it clear that they are related to the people whose acquaintance we shall make more fully at Bologna. The cremating tribes who preceded the Etruscans everywhere belong to a single great family and their civilization is closely related. But there are some differences of local habit north and south of the Apennines, so that it is useful to see collections from both sides of the mountains. Here in Etruria one of the peculiarities of the Villanovans is that they generally cover their cremation urns with a helmet. Often it is a pottery imitation but sometimes, as in the fine group which stands in the centre of the room, it is a real bronze helmet of admirable workmanship. The Villanovans were quite good bronze-workers even before the Etruscans arrived with their superior skill and technique.

The three cemeteries which yielded the objects

seen in this room run from the tenth century to the
eighth. It is curious to note that weapons are very
rare, evidently metals were not nearly so abundant as after the Etruscan development of the
mines. The pottery is primitive hand-made ware,
mostly of the coarse black fabric which was the
ancestor of true bucchero. But one group of
tombs produced wheel-made ware of a different
clay, which was obviously imported. And as all
the people buried in this particular group used
a different burial rite, inhumation instead of
cremation, it is clear that they belonged to a small
colony of immigrant potters.

Orvieto is placed under the title ' Volsinienses ',
and it is generally accepted now that ' Volsinii
veteres ' was really Orvieto. The later Volsinii
was on the Lago di Bolsena, near which was the
Fanum Voltumnae, described by Livy as the
meeting-place of the heads of the Confederation.
The finest thing in this room is the archaic head
of a warrior carved in stone, which has been
already mentioned in a previous chapter. To the
end of the sixth century belong some painted Attic
vases. The gilded bronze armour from a tomb at
Sette Camini is of the fourth century, and some
pottery heads, as well as the terra-cotta revetments
of a temple, belong to the same period.

From the topographically arranged rooms on

the ground floor we pass to the upper floor, where objects are arranged more by subject than by place. Here it will be well to conclude our study of Chiusi by going straight into the large room which is entirely filled with the well-known black bucchero pottery. Chiusi was one of the principal centres of its manufacture, though it was distributed widely all over the country, and there was quite a notable development of it as far south as Campania. The invention of this handsome ware is due to the Etruscan improvement on a technique which was many centuries old before they arrived. Black pottery had been made all over the peninsula, by a very simple process which I have tested by experiment. Primitive man did not use a kiln but an open bonfire, which produced a great deal of smoke and burned at a comparatively low temperature. The percolation of the smoke through the clay will turn it to a glossy black. All that the Etruscans did was to use a much finer clay, and whenever possible to select a kind that contained manganese. If the manganese was not already present they probably added it. If they used kilns they must have been careful to keep the temperature fairly low, as otherwise the black being principally due to carbon will burn out to red. In the fashioning of the pottery the Etruscans used the wheel and acquired a great dexterity.

The chronological grading of the different styles is less simple than it may appear at the first glance, and a good deal of allowance must be made for local variation. The finest specimens are of the seventh and sixth centuries, before the increased importations of Greek pottery drove bucchero out of favour.

Leaving out of consideration the fine collection of Greek vases which has nothing to do with our present purpose, and giving no more than a glance to the famous painted sarcophagus of the third century with its battle of the Amazons, because it is so essentially Greek as to lie outside our present range, we should concentrate attention on the stone carvings and the bronze statues and statuettes.

In Room XXI are several stone sarcophagi of great interest. One from Orvieto in archaic style, but no doubt rightly attributed to the sixth century, has a roof-shaped lid and is ornamented with carved masks, and with figures of a lion and two griffins. Another from the same place is carved with twin figures of goddesses of the lower world.

Several cinerary chests from Chiusi give representations of the Etruscan houses; one of these which has often been reproduced has Tuscan columns at the angles and a roofed loggia. Another has Ionic columns, arched doors, and a roofed loggia, in a style which recalls all the essential

H

features of a palace of the Renaissance. Milani remarks that it might really almost be called the prototype of the Riccardi palace, built for the Medici by Michelozzo, and familiar to every visitor who makes his pilgrimage to see the paintings of Benozzo Gozzoli. Still another shows the entrance of a tomb flanked by its cypresses, with the deceased person saying farewell to his relatives. The elaborate architecture of some districts is further illustrated by the fragment of a façade from Norchia where the entrances were sculptured like temples.

Two statues of very primitive form from Chiusi are almost shapeless except for the heads, which are carved to represent the Great Mother and her daughter, the Etruscan equivalent of Persephone. A late sarcophagus of polychrome terra-cotta, also from Chiusi, bears the name of Larthia Seianti, daughter of Svenia, and shows the dress of a great lady in the second century B.C. We may note the diadem of verbena, the bracelets, necklace, and earrings, and the little red shoes with jewelled fastenings.

A room given up to small bronze objects of art contains many beautiful pieces of minor tomb furniture, *situlae*, candelabra, and censers of various dates. The art of the fourth and third centuries, of which I have said but little, may be

13. THE BRONZE CHIMAERA FROM AREZZO

studied in the finds from Telamone and Todi. Some of the helmets and weapons from other places are also worthy of attention. But for the main lines of principal development it is more important to visit the Sala delle Statue. Here, with dozens of exquisite minor pieces, statuettes of Mars and Vertumnus, Minerva, Hercules, and others, are three or four great masterpieces, landmarks in the history of Etruscan sculpture.

First in dramatic effect and originality of conception no less than in the perfection of its technique I should place the Chimaera of Arezzo. It is only second in quality to the Apollo of Veii, though much later, belonging to the third or possibly the fourth century B.C. Except for two of the legs which were restored by Benvenuto Cellini, and for the serpent tail which was added later, it is complete and no less marvellous to-day than when it was discovered in 1553. The Chimaera is a glorious creature, a conception as imaginative as any dragon by Piero di Cosimo, and far superior in fire-breathing quality to the tame beasts of Carpaccio, which were ready to be converted to Christianity after defeat by St. George. Zoologically I believe it is true to type, as though Hesiod's description of a chimaera is rather question-begging, the later writers decided that the creature should have the front of a lion and the tail of a serpent, with the head of a goat in the middle. The goat's head is represented as already dying, fatally wounded by the spear of Bellerophon. Benvenuto Cellini refers to the discovery of this, and some other bronzes which unfortunately cannot be identified, in a passage of his *Life* (ii. 87). Cosimo dei Medici entrusted him with restoring it. It is thought that it may have formed part of a group in which Bellerophon was the chief figure (Plate 13).

The Chimaera of Arezzo should be compared with another bronze animal, well known even in the Middle Ages, namely, the famous Wolf of the Capitol now in the Palazzo dei Conservatori at Rome. It is mentioned by a tenth-century writer as standing in the Lateran palace, from which it was removed to the Capitol in 1471.

Less original, as it is so obviously derived from a Greek model, is the Minerva, also discovered at Arezzo in 1554, that is to say, one year after the Chimaera. The type and style are Greek of the fifth century.

Far more remarkable than these echoes of Greek masters is the great bronze Arringatore or Orator found near Lake Trasimene. It was dedicated, as its Etruscan inscription shows, to Aulus Metellus, son of Vesia, and may be dated to about 300 B.C. This is not Greek in its conception; it is

14. THE ORATOR

A bronze statue from Lake Trasimene

an independent work which shows the origin of the Roman school of portrait sculpture. The Etruscan advocate, clothed in toga and pallium, is shown with his arm upraised in the act of peroration. For vividness and naturalism of face and gesture this work is unsurpassed.

CHAPTER 7

Etrusco-mania and the reaction from it ; The earliest art is
not influenced by Greece but by Asia and the Levant ; The
Etruscans inherited artistic taste and skill ; Their work was
often independent and original ; Greek influence only
begins in the seventh century but then rapidly begins to
dominate ; The architecture, however, is not of Greek origin ; Native schools of sculpture, especially the school of
Vulca ; Independence of Etruscan genius maintained even
in later days.

THE study of the Etruscans—Etruscology if
it might be so called—is not at all a modern
development. As early as 1616 the Scottish baro-
net Sir Thomas Dempster, Professor of Law at
Pisa, wrote an erudite work called *De Etruria regali
libri septem* which was published a century later
with notes by Filippo Buonarotti. All through the
eighteenth century there was much activity in research and discovery, which led to the foundation
of various learned societies and museums. This
gradually produced a most mischievous habit of
mind in a world that was quite ignorant of the
range and variety of archaeology. It may be called
Etrusco-mania. For some generations it was fashion-
able to attribute the origin of everything that was
interesting or valuable in ancient civilization to
the Etruscans, and to assume that they were the
masters of the Greeks and the equals of the

Egyptians. Echoes of these fallacies may still be found in popular books, and there are many innocent people who still imagine that painted vases clearly signed with the names of Athenian artists were produced by the Etruscans. This exaggeration of course brought its own punishment; scholars soon redressed the balance and acquired a truer scale of values. But of late years there has been considerable danger that the pendulum might swing too far in the opposite direction. The knowledge and study of Greek archaeology has spread far and wide, and has occupied many of the best minds, while Italian subjects have been relegated to the background. Hence there has been a tendency to regard all Italian civilization as a derivation or an imitation from the Greek, and the possibility of its independence has been ignored. In the case of the Etruscans it has been all the easier to do this because in some periods they were obviously dominated by Greek influence, but the subject has seldom been approached impartially. Even our best art critics of to-day are strongly pro-Hellenic in their bias. Ionian creation is assumed rather than proved for every work of archaic art, and every spark of originality is denied to a people who, even in antiquity, were universally recognized as possessing conspicuous artistic genius.

It would be ridiculous to deny the existence of a very strong Greek influence on the Etruscans, and I have no wish to minimize its importance. But there are two considerations which have been ignored, and which I wish to emphasize—perhaps almost for the first time. The first is that it is essential to distinguish between periods, and to recognize that there was a long and important stage during which any foreign element that acted upon the Etruscans was not Greek; it was what I have called near-Asiatic.

The second is that in the sixth century and afterwards, when Greek influence was undoubtedly very strong, the native genius may often have asserted itself in the production of works that are truly original, though their authors may have trained themselves on foreign models. A Whistler or a Sargent may study in Paris, but it does not follow that his work should be classed as French.

I will now develop these two themes more at length. First, then, it is absolutely unhistorical to suggest that there is any appreciable Greek current in Etruscan work of any kind before the middle of the seventh century. A very active commerce had been proceeding for a hundred or a hundred and fifty years before this between Etruria and the Aegean. But all the rich contents of princely graves in the eighth and early seventh

centuries show that the trade was with Phoeni-
cians, Cypriotes, Syrians, and other peoples who
were swarming round a crucible of Egypto-
Assyrian civilization situated somewhere in the
Levant. It would be impossible for any one
familiar with art of the Regolini, Bernardini, and
Barberini graves to maintain that it is Greek.
Any objects of the early seventh century which
are demonstrably imported from abroad show
an inspiration which is originally derived almost
equally from Egypt and from Assyria, worked out
in an atmosphere and surroundings which belong
to neither country. Exactly at what points on the
littoral of Asia Minor, Syria, or even the islands,
the principal laboratories of this new hybrid art
may have been situated we cannot yet detect;
everything seems to indicate a centre fairly equidistant from Egypt and Mesopotamia, but we must
wait for more knowledge of Asia Minor and the
nearer East before attempting to define more
closely.

Next I must point out that, whereas no doubt
the Etruscans imported freely, yet they themselves
must have been very fine craftsmen at the time
when they landed in Italy. A colonist may be a
pioneer but he is seldom a dunce; he is generally
a very able man. In modern days his abilities are
likely to be concentrated on agriculture, but the

prime need of the first colonists in Etruria was mining and metal-work. It is only natural, then, that skilled copper-workers and smiths should have formed a part of the very first crews that left Asia. This has been almost universally forgotten or ignored. The long prevalence of the false conception that the Etruscans were a barbarous horde coming in over the Alps has misled the past generation of scholars and historians; they have not yet cast off its incubus and grasped all the implications of the new theory. But if the Asiatic origin of the Etruscans is admitted it must also be admitted that they came from a country of very ancient and deep-rooted civilization, whether this country was Lydia, Lycia, or some neighbouring province. Situated as they had been mid-way between all the great empires of antiquity, they must have experienced centuries of schooling. The perfect command of all the technique of metal-work, whether in bronze, iron, silver, or gold, which appears in the very earliest graves of this people at Vetulonia, shows a facility that necessarily presupposes many generations of apprenticeship. For it cannot possibly be maintained that everything in the abundant deposits of 750 to 650 B.C. is imported. It would be preposterous to suppose that many tons of ready worked bronze and iron, including such bulky

objects as chariots, and thrones, and beds, cauldrons, shields, and innumerable dishes and bowls,
were shipped over hundreds of miles of sea to
furnish the tomb of every wealthy man. The
greater part of all this tomb equipment, and the
greater part of all the metal-work so prodigally
used at this period, must have been produced in
Tuscany, near the very place where the mines were
being so actively exploited. Moreover, if a certain
number of models, prize pieces perhaps of
Asiatic craftsmen, were imported, why should
they not have come from the old homeland in
Lydia or wherever it was? What more natural
than to suppose that they were made by the
cousins and relatives and fellow townsmen of the
Tyrrheni whom they had left behind them? Now
and again we may imagine too that a few dozen
Tyrrhene artificers, finding that work was scarce
at home, might feel inclined to try their fortunes
in the new countries of the west; just as skilled
workmen in our own days may be tempted to join
the cousin who is so prosperous in America. But
they were not setting out to join a colony of
illiterate boors; on the contrary they were going
to make a better living and find higher wages
among some of the most progressive and able of
their own countrymen. It is in my opinion a
totally false conception to suppose that the princes

of Corneto and Caere and Vetulonia had to wait
for cargoes from the East to bring them everything
but the barest necessities of life. Like our own
old East India or China merchants, like the old
traders of Salem and Boston, they might delight in
the newest products of the Oriental market, but
they had an ample supply of fine things made by
their own workmen in their own country; however pleasant it might be to vary the fashions, and
to enrich their already wealthy homes with various
and rare objects from abroad.

So considerable, indeed, was the amount of
native manufacture that by the early seventh
century the Etruscans were producing for export,
and it is not too much to suppose that they had
conquered a considerable foreign market. It is
certain at any rate that great bronze cauldrons
such as I have described and illustrated were
thought worthy of being dedicated at Olympia,
and a great man in the Greek colony of Cumae
could actually equip his tomb with bronzes indistinguishable from those which I have described
at Caere and Praeneste. All through the eighth
century, and the beginning of the seventh, the
goldsmiths of Vetulonia were steadily perfecting
an art which their fathers must have learned as
apprentices before they left the Levant. Beginning
with a purely geometrical style, which looks simple

but demands when used in goldwork an extraordinary mastery of technical procedure, they modified their designs to suit the new fashions which began to come into vogue about 700 B.C. This is the beginning of mythological scenes, with figures of men and animals. Like the painters of Giotto's school they were now emancipating themselves from an age-old formalism. And the jewellery of Vetulonia was also exported, finding its way sometimes up to the simple barbarians in Romagna across the Apennines.

This process, then, of developing a near-Asiatic art on Italian soil, enriching it with new grafts and forming it into a new and independent growth, had been in progress for a century and a half before any specifically Greek influence began to be felt. It is this point which has been totally ignored by historians and archaeologists. But about 650 B.C. a new current can be clearly distinguished, which gains in strength and breadth till it becomes a flood a hundred years later. In the middle of the seventh century new forces had come to the front in the commerce of the Aegean, and their influence had begun to be reflected in Etruria. Between 650 and 600 Corinth is forging to the front, becoming the most powerful and productive centre of manufacture and export in the Eastern Mediterranean. In Southern Italy the colonies of Magna Graecia are firmly established and afford a ready market for Greek products, which naturally overflow into Etruria. Ships sailing to Cumae, the most important and influential of all the Greek cities in Italy at this time, could easily prolong their voyage to ports on the Tyrrhene coast, or disembark them at Naples, whence they could be carried in Cumaean bottoms. For it is to be observed that the commercial routes were not overland but always by sea; also that no traffic went up the Adriatic, which was a closed sea, probably owing to piracy. The commerce of the seventh century was at first limited principally to such small commodities, unguents, medicaments, spices, or whatever they might be, as could be carried in little pots, Corinthian aryballoi, and balsamaries. As Corinth becomes more important, however, her larger decorative pottery is extensively imported, handsome wares decorated with fantastic orientalizing animals and figures. But there are no Ionic bronzes, for it is useless to send coals to Newcastle or worked bronze to Etruria. Ivory, however, was not native in Italy, so it is natural that ivory *situlae* like those of Chiusi should be of foreign workmanship. Early in the sixth century the Attic wares appear, beginning with the great François vase of Chiusi, which is in itself a complete mythological dictionary for those who wish to learn the names of Greek story. Then for a hundred years the products of the Athenian potters flood the country until every Greek god and every Greek hero has become a household name. And not only manufactures but workmen come in numbers, if we accept Ducati's good suggestion that the oppression of the Ionians by Persia in the sixth century drove many of them to emigrate to Italy. It was like the spread of the New Learning in the fifteenth century after Christ when the Turks had taken Constantinople.

It was a natural result that Greek influence should be entirely dominant in many minor arts as well as in painting, in regard to which I have already stated that the Etruscan frescoes owe everything to a style derived from Corinthian and Athenian vase painters. So long as we are only speaking of these minor arts and of painting there can be little objection to the usual statement, that from the sixth century onwards Greek and Etruscan work in Italy are virtually indistinguishable. But this judgement must not be too hastily applied to the major arts of architecture and sculpture, which need to be discussed separately.

Etruscan architecture is a difficult subject which needs to be worked out with careful attention to dates if we are to arrive at reliable results. The most puzzling thing is that though there are numerous burials there is no tomb architecture earlier than 700 B.C. For a hundred years or more, to judge from the site of Vetulonia, the finest graves were nothing more elaborate than rings of stone slabs mounded over with earth. It is only just about 700 B.C. that immense and costly tumuli are found in widely separated regions, Vetulonia, Caere, Cortona, even Fabriano. I think it is most natural to regard these as an evolution of the Vetulonia circles, products of the self-taught science of naturally inventive men. If they recall great structures in Asia Minor like the tomb of Alyattes as described by Herodotus it is not necessary to infer that they were imitated from unknown buildings which we do not even know to have really existed in 700 B.C. Indeed, though the theory of Dennis and other writers that the Etruscans brought over a system of architecture ready formed from Asia Minor is extremely plausible, it is very hard to reconcile with the archaeological facts so far as they are known at present. The same difficulty occurs in regard to the false arches and false vaults used in the approaches and interior chambers of some tumuli. The Regolini-Galassi has a corridor and chamber roofed by the primitive method of overlapping courses; the Pietrera and Diavolino at Vetulonia show the same system applied to a conical roof, resulting in a regular tholos. We are inevitably reminded of certain beehive tombs in Crete and Greece, but the dates are very difficult to reconcile with any direct connexion. After all these early systems of building are common to man the world over from ' China to Peru ', or more literally from Mexico to Egypt. So that, as far as any judgement can be given on the tomb architecture of the seventh century, it would seem likely that the Etruscans had worked out an independent system of their own, with an occasional hint perhaps from their Asiatic kinsmen. From the sixth century onwards the wealthier type of tomb generally reproduces in its interior more or less the structure of the contemporary house ; apart from the frescoes there is no particularly Greek note, except for some accessory ornament about the capitals and doorways. In some places, but by no means universally, there is an imitation of foreign forms in the sculptured façades, as at Castel d'Asso and Norchia.

Temples are of purely native character, if we put aside the terra-cotta revetments, which belong rather to sculpture than architecture. It is possible to judge of them by remains which come down to the fifth century. The temples were very simple constructions of crude brick and timber ; it was not till the fourth century that they were built of stone. It is obviously irrelevant to suggest a Greek origin for these rustic buildings, with their triple sanctuaries designed for purely Etruscan gods. Houses, moreover, as I have said in speaking of the models found at Chiusi, are entirely Italian in character and design. In short, Hellenic influence when it comes into Etruria plays principally upon the externals, it does not penetrate to the essentials of life. Language, religion, manners, and domestic habits remain Etruscan from first to last.

Sculpture only began to come into existence about 700 B.C. The rough stone carvings of La Pietrera at Vetulonia show how rudimentary it still was at that date. But in its beginnings it is purely native without any foreign note. Primitive statues like those of the Primoli ossuary, gravestones like those of Larthi Atharnies, represent the earliest efforts of self-taught artists. A number of bas-reliefs carved in soft stone show gradual progression during the seventh century, and the pottery heads of the Chiusi ' Canopics ' prove that the local artists had become capable of doing admirable modelling before the sixth century. There was, then, in some parts of the country at least a real school of indigenous sculpture long before any Ionic influence could possibly appear. This is an important consideration when we come to estimate the effect and the range of archaic

Greek art in the sixth century. The one great example of this period is the Apollo of Veii, which must stand as the type of a whole school, the famous school of the Veientines. And my question is how far is this the product of Etruscan genius or how far is it a masterly imitation of lost Greek originals? Now first of all I have shown that there were certain schools of Etruscan sculpture already in existence, and secondly I must point out that the Veientine school itself was certainly much older than 520 or 510, the presumable date of this Apollo. For the mere technique of execution, the superb modelling, the very difficult process of burning these great terra-cotta masses in kilns specially made for the purpose, all presuppose long years of training and apprenticeship. There must have been fine terra-cotta statues at Veii long before 500 B.C.

On the other hand those who argue for the Greek origin of this school may point to the fact that the very subject is a Greek myth.

Here I must leave the question, to be solved by each person according to his aesthetic feeling; the historical probabilities seem to be equally balanced, my object has been to show that they are not overwhelmingly on the side of Greek origin. To me the whole conception of the god is purely Etruscan, the feeling is un-Hellenic, the remorseless terrible deity is the very incarnation of what I should feel an Etruscan god to have been. And if I am right then the works of Vulca that adorned the Capitoline temple were not mere echoes of some Ionian master, they were true expressions of that Etruscan religion which was the official religion of Rome itself.

From the fifth century onwards there was no doubt a great deal of quite deliberate copying of Greek masterpieces. An obvious example of this type is the great Minerva of Arezzo, and doubtless there were hundreds of others. This has nothing to do with my present purpose, for they tell us nothing about the Etruscans. What does interest me, however, is to point out that the native genius was not atrophied by the manufacture of copies, original work could still be produced. The superb statue of the Arringatore or Orator in the Florence Museum shows the powerful spirit of originality which was asserting itself about 300 B.C. The Capitoline wolf is the product of technical skill of the highest order; the Chimaera is more, it is a superb work of imagination. But the Orator, an outburst of pure spontaneity, has a special interest, for it marks the beginnings of a school which was the parent of Roman portrait-sculpture. The sculptors of the Roman Empire owe less to the Greeks than to the Etruscans.

CHAPTER 8

Brevity of inscriptions and small hope of information from them; The Agram mummy; Vain search for affinities of the language; The Alphabet and its derivation; Absence of literature; Divining; Deities and religion; Ideas of the future life; Pictures of death and the underworld.

UP to this point I have said nothing about the writing and hardly anything about the language of the Etruscans. In fact I was not sorry to demonstrate that we can know a good deal about them without using these factors, which have a certain value for the archaeologist, but far less than the ordinary layman would suppose. It would be different of course if there were the slightest hope that we might ever find documents telling anything of Etruscan life and customs. But the amount of material is so small that it can hardly give any appreciable amount of information on any subject, and the only subjects on which it may conceivably throw light are those which have comparatively slight importance for the history of civilization. There was something more than flippancy in the reply made to a person who had been reading a newspaper puff of the achievements of a philologist previously, and ever since, unknown to fame. ' I see that the key to Etruscan has been discovered,' said this person. And the reply was : ' I am really not greatly interested in the key to a door which opens an empty room.' In this instance it was sufficiently well known to most people that the key was the work of an ignorant bungler, and would never open anything.

Very eminent philologists have devoted their best abilities for a long while past to the study of the Etruscan language, and if they have so far been baffled it is not the fault of their science but of the lack of material. It may be true that there are between 8,000 and 9,000 so-called inscriptions in existence, but they are almost all so short that they would reduce to a very small number of pages if printed consecutively. There are seldom more than a few words in any inscription; the most usual form of those which are least useless is a brief epitaph, consisting of a name, a statement of relationship, and the number of years of the life. There are only nine inscriptions which contain anything like thirty words apiece ; it is obvious that they cannot convey much information even when they are deciphered.

Actually the longest document was found in a most unexpected place and has a very curious history. It is written on the linen wrappings of a mummy found in Alexandria in Egypt and is now in the museum of Agram. It is said to contain 1,500 words, which, with allowance made for constant repetitions, are reduced in reality to about 500. It is a fair inference from the names of gods, which seem to occur very frequently, as well as from the circumstances of its finding, that the Agram document is of religious character. Possibly it contains extracts from some of the books of the lower world, ' Acherontian books ' as the Roman writers called them ; but there can be little certainty even of this, for who can say if an Etruscan buried in Egypt was loyally following the creed of his people? He may have become a proselyte to the religion of the country in which he was domiciled.

It is extraordinarily dangerous to prophesy in regard to discovery, but it seems almost safe to say that we shall never receive much direct light on the events of history from any Etruscan inscription.

There is one direction, however, in which philology may render an important service, and in which tangible results of value may be obtained almost any day. This is in establishing the relationship and connexions of the Etruscan language. One real advance has been made which is perfectly consistent with everything that I have written from the archaeological side. With very few exceptions the best philologists are all agreed that Etruscan is not an Indo-European language, and it follows that it has no relationship to Latin

or any ancient Italian dialect. This entirely cor-
roborates the view to which we have been driven
by all the archaeological evidence, namely, that the
Etruscans are foreigners of a different stock from
any of the earlier inhabitants of Italy.

What the real affiliations of the language may
be no one has yet discovered. Searches have been
made in the most improbable places as well as the
most probable. Every kind of wild suggestion has
been mentioned. I believe it has not yet been
suggested that Etruscan was the language of the
Lost Tribes; the dates would be somewhat difficult to harmonize, but this need prove no
obstacle to a real enthusiast. Almost every other
possibility and impossibility has been suggested.
The disappointing thing is that serious research
by really scientific philologists has so far brought
no result from Asia Minor. Of course the available
material for comparison is very slight, the number
of inscriptions from Sardis is inconsiderable, and it
is always possible that any new site may suddenly
produce an unsuspected series. Somewhere between the Hellespont on the north and Syria on
the south the parent language must have existed,
if only it could be discovered. Possibly it may be
on some one of the islands; the nearest relationship yet known seems to be an inscription from
Lemnos. Almost any year the progress of explora-

tion may give the clue. To the archaeologist it does not matter greatly what the particular province may be, whether it is Lydia, Lycia, or another, provided it be within the general area already mentioned. We accept the tradition given by Herodotus in its broad lines, but do not necessarily subscribe to the details. In order to have a convenient name I have spoken of the Etruscans as Lydians; but it would make no difference to anything that has been said if they should turn out to be Lycians, Phrygians, Mysians, or even Hittites. All that is required is that they should have lived somewhere within the focus of what I have styled the near-Asiatic civilization, compounded of a medley of elements derived at second or third hand from Egypt and Mesopotamia, with a predominance of the Mesopotamian factor.

If the origin of the language offers difficulties which have hitherto proved insuperable, the origin of the alphabet is perfectly clear. It is a variant of an alphabet probably older than scholars have generally supposed, which was also used by the Greeks. I deliberately do not say that it was invented by the Greeks, though this is a common view. Until very recently all writers assumed as a matter of course that the Etruscans derived it from Cumae. The assumption belongs to that habit of mind which could not imagine that anything Etruscan was not borrowed from some Greek source. It is very satisfactory, therefore, that this facile theory should have been exploded by the most recent research. It has now been proved that the Etruscan alphabet contains letters not used by the Campanian Greeks, and represents an older inheritance of independent evolution. Accordingly we need not hesitate to suppose that it was brought over as an already completed and familiar instrument by the first batch of Asiatic immigrants. I have mentioned several of the earliest instances of its use, and am indebted to Karo for the interesting remark that the f sound in the name of Avtilés Feluskés is expressed by a letter found also in the Lydian alphabet, though it is not in the Cumaean. Apart from the names on these two or three very early gravestones, the earliest inscription on Italian soil occurs on a bucchero vase in the Tomb of the Prince at Vetulonia. Of the alphabet written out complete in the consecutive order of its letters there are three very early versions, one of which on the ivory tablet of Marsiliana can be dated to a few years after 700 B.C. The other two are inscribed on earthenware pots, found respectively near Veii (Formello) and at Caere, which may be seen in the Villa Giulia Museum and in the Vatican Museum at Rome. I reproduce, from

Ducati's *Etruria antica*, a table of the three versions, with the corresponding sounds in Italian values. It is to be observed that the equivalents of several consonants are not Greek but are much closer to Semitic. The three versions agree very closely, but in the Formello alphabet the fifth and sixth letters are inverted from the order which they hold as sixth and fifth at Marsiliana and Cervetri.

The comparative rarity and brevity of inscriptions might be easily explained by supposing that as the language was foreign it was not used by the majority of the people, whereas the great nobles, though not illiterate, were occupied with a number of things more useful than writing. It is not every one that handles a pen as a matter of course. From the absence of allusions in the Latin writers it is naturally inferred that there was very little Etruscan literature of any kind. Poetry and the drama seem to have been unknown. Religious books were only composed at a quite late stage, and it may be supposed that for a long while it was deemed neither politic nor useful to commit to writing that esoteric learning which was the special property of the priests. By the time of Julius Caesar, however, the general outlines of an ' Etrusca disciplina ' were well known, and they were freely discussed not only by Cicero but by several of his contemporaries. It is possible that

	Marsiliana	Formello	Cervetri	
1.	A	A	A	= a
2.	ꓭ	B	ꓭ	= b
3.	ꓶ	‹	C	= g
4.	◁	D	D	= d
5.	⊐	F	E	= e
6.	ꓱ	E	F	= f
7.	I	I	I	= z
8.	⊟	⊟	⊟	= h
9.	⊗	⊕	⊗	= th
10.	I	I	I	= i
11.	ꓘ	K	K	= k
12.	ꓩ	ꓸ	ꓸ	= l
13.	ꟽ	ꟽ	••••	= m
14.	ꓦ	N	M	= n
15.	⊞	⊞	⊞	= s
16.	O	⊙	⊙	= o
17.	ꓶ	P	P	= p
18.	M	M	ꓦ	= s
19.	ꝯ	ꝯ	••••	= q
20.	ꝗ	P	P	= r
21.	ꙅ	ꙗ	ꙗ	= s
22.	T	ꓩ	T	= t
23.	ꓬ	ꓬ	ꓬ	= y
24.	X	X	X	= cs
25.	Φ	Φ	P	= ph
26.	Ψ	Ψ	Ψ	= ch

Three versions of the Earliest Etruscan
Alphabet

the monumental work of the Emperor Claudius embodied a great deal of learning on this subject.

One side of the Etruscan religion has a great interest from the point of view of origins. This is the practice of divining by the livers of sheep, which is certainly derived from Chaldaea. Models of clay livers from Mesopotamia inscribed in cuneiform show exactly the same system that is used on the bronze model of a liver found at Piacenza. The liver is divided up by lines into sections, in each of which is written the name of a deity who is to preside over that particular part. The Roman haruspices inherited this method, and used to examine the liver to see whether it was sound in all its parts, or whether some diseased section showed that a particular deity was un-favourable. A similar principle was applied to the reading of the heavens, just as it is now practised by any modern ' astrologer '. Divining by the flight of birds is another Eastern practice which was used by the Etruscans and has become familiar in Roman history and literature.

Of the principles of the religion, however, it is difficult to obtain much understanding, for the mere names of a few divinities do not convey any information as to their character and functions. The religion of the ruling classes must have been something very different from that of the indigenous country folk, whether in Etruria or in Latium. Certain unifications were made for political purposes, thus Tinia was identified with Jupiter, Uni with Juno, Menrva with Minerva; and in this fusion it is easy to see that at least two out of the three gods in the Capitoline triad are derived from the Etruscan. Besides these the names of many other deities have been transmitted by the inscriptions, one of the most important being Voltumna, known to the Romans as Vertumnus, whose principal shrine was on the lake of Bolsena.

But, unless a series of religious texts should some day be discovered and interpreted, we must renounce all hope of making anything like a systematic study of the religion. It is only within recent years that scholars, who have had a mass of literature to aid them, have succeeded in unravelling the difficult and obscure subject of the Latin religion. And as this in turn is something very different from the Greek, and quite unlike the formalized scheme handed down by writers of the Augustan age, it is quite evident that the Etruscan system must be beyond our ken. Probably, however, it was a *system*, and in this it differed from the episodical and unsystematic religion of the Latins. It would be quite interesting to speculate whether perhaps, underneath the crystallized forms of ritual and mythology derived from Chaldaea, there may not have persisted some primitive natural beliefs common to all the tribes of Italian stock, brought from their original Danubian homes. If it is possible to detect any vestiges of these in modern folk-lore they would be survivals from an early stratum, lying far beneath the superficial uniformity imposed by the ruling race.

From the pictures in the frescoes of the tombs a certain amount may be inferred as to the ideas of a future life. As with so many ancient peoples, in the Mediterranean and elsewhere, this was regarded as more or less a repetition of the existence in this world. Herein lies the motive for burying in the grave so many personal ornaments, weapons, and objects of all kinds used by their owner in his lifetime, as well as models and imitations of things which he may not have actually used but would certainly like to possess. This is also supposed to be the explanation of the subjects of the frescoes. For they are not mainly commemorative or biographical; that is to say, they were seldom intended to record amusements, banquets, sports, and games as past events, but rather to ensure by a sort of sympathetic magic the repetition of these happy moments in the afterworld. It is the same practice that is very general in the Egyptian tomb paintings.

In an earlier chapter I have spoken of the

Etruscan frescoes at Corneto and other places, and have remarked that whereas those of the earlier period are happy and cheerful in their atmosphere, those of the later times are gloomy and overcast with a certain brooding sense of terror. Some writers rather fancifully suggest that this latter mood reflects the depressed feelings of a people no longer triumphant but conquered and dejected. The gay scenes of festivals and banquets, they say, are symptoms of a time of careless prosperity, while the others betray a phase when the consciousness of failure is oppressing the mind of the community. This seems to me exaggerated and unnatural. It is much simpler to suppose that at some periods the fashion was to lay more stress on the happy episodes of life, and in others to emphasize the grimness and inevitable horror of death. No psychological revolution is necessary. Precisely the same contrast may be seen, even within a single period, in Italian churches, where the exquisite paganism of the Renaissance jostles the brutal realism of the less poetic minds. In one chapel there will be ugly skeletons, death heads, and worms about the tomb, in another scenes so joyous and smiling that they fill the spectator with delight.

Actually if they are examined the Etruscan scenes are not really so terrifying as they are described, and not a whit worse than those in many a Christian church. If grim Charun is there with his mallet I find him no more unpleasant than Death or Father Time with his scythe, whom you may see in any village in England. Nowhere in Etruria do we find the nightmare fancies of hideous and obscene creatures that may be seen in royal tombs in Egypt, when the soul not precisely equipped with the correct formulae is made the prey of every terror. Some idea of punishment and reward there seems to be, at least in the later periods ; it is suggested by scenes in the ' Tomb of the Cardinal ' and the ' Tomb of Orcus ' at Corneto, produced under the influence of Pythagorean Greeks. But nowhere, except perhaps in the Tomba Tartaglia, is there any approach to that appalling realism, and sheer gloating over torture, in which the Christian Middle Ages found such delight. Dante and Orcagna are far more terrifying and far more cruel ; and yet their savage moods did not cloud the joyous life of fourteenth-century Tuscany. The Etruscans may not have possessed all the serenity of the Hellenic spirit, but there is no reason at all to think of them as living in a hag-ridden atmosphere like the witch-burners of Salem.

Many of them doubtless hoped that the same good fortune would befall them which came to one of the Velii, who died and travelled correctly down to the underworld in his chariot, as shown in a fresco at Sette Camini near Orvieto. He arrived in the midst of a most cheerful banquet spread for all the members of his family. Their own servants were there preparing the food and handing the wine, while the pipe-players assiduously played ' The Campbells are coming ' or the equivalent Etruscan tune. And the gods of the underworld, like good fellows, were smilingly taking their part in the feast. So it was on this day and so it might continue interminably.

CHAPTER 9

Etruscan colonies in the north; Bologna and its pre-Etruscan population; Civilization of the Villanovans; Effect of Etruscan inspiration and organization in Italy; Other pre-Etruscan peoples in Umbria and Picenum; Campania; Extent of Etruscan influence in Italy.

IT was in the last years of the sixth century that the Etruscans, then at the height of their political power, felt themselves strong enough to send out colonies which established themselves on the north of the Apennines. One of the first and always the most important of these was Felsina, on the site of Bologna, where a cluster of small towns or villages of the native Villanovans had long existed. On a high plateau above Felsina, about seventeen miles away, was built Marzabotto, to protect the road over the mountains and secure communications with the nearest town in Etruria proper, Fiesole or, as it was then called, Faesulae.

This was intended to be the beginning of a new Etruria, which should include the whole basin of the Po and extend out to the shores of the Adriatic. To a considerable extent this dream seems to have been fulfilled; and but for the invasions of the Gauls which burst upon them at the beginning of the fourth century, the power of the Etruscans would have been consolidated all over this region up to the Alps, except for Venetia. From the Venetian corner of the peninsula, as Livy states and archaeology amply proves, they were always excluded. The reason was that all this north-eastern region was held by a very vigorous and independent people distantly related to the Villanovans, who had planted themselves near Padova at Este, which was then a flourishing port on the navigable Adige. The Etruscans placed their own port at Hatria or Adria, which has given its name to the Adriatic, between the delta of the Po and the mouth of the Adige. Farther south near Comacchio was also established a place called Spina, which served as the principal port of Felsina.

Livy speaks of ' Etruria circumpadana ' as composed of twelve colonies, corresponding to the twelve cities of the Etruscan confederation south of the Apennines, but they have not been traced, and there are some doubts whether they ever existed. The most western settlement was somewhere near Milan, at the place called Melpo, which must have been a border town as it was the first victim of the Gauls. Archaeological discovery has shown a certain amount of Etruscan influence round the Italian lakes in the fifth century, but not more than could be explained as the

effects of trade. It seems in fact a fair inference
from the scantiness of the remains that there was
never any very effective domination of Lombardy,
though there was a great deal of trade through
Bellinzona to the Rhine. Felsina on the site of
Bologna has been very completely explored. The
Etruscan city has yielded a very large collection
of red-figured Athenian pottery, numerous stelae
of the fifth century, and many minor objects, few
of which, however, are of first-rate importance for
the history of art. Except for the Certosa *situla*,
which I have so fully discussed in the second
chapter, the Museo Civico contains little to compare with the fine work of Etruria proper, though
there is a great deal that a specialist may study
with advantage.

The great interest of the Bolognese site is that
it has given the *coup de grâce* to several baseless
theories in regard to the origin of the Etruscans.
The proof that Felsina was not founded before the
end of the sixth century shows the impossibility
of Niebuhr's idea that the invaders came over the
Alps. And the proof that the Etruscan cemetery
is on a wholly different site from the Villanovan,
separated from the latter by a clear space of fifty-
six metres and a wide boundary ditch, shows that
the Etruscans were not a mere evolution from a
native Italian people. Ample evidence has been

already adduced in the preceding chapters on both these points, but the Bolognese excavations must settle the last doubts if any persist. They demonstrate the late arrival of the Etruscans in the valley of the Po, and they show that the Etruscans were preceded by an Italian race, who occupied this area from about 1000 B.C. until after 500 B.C. when they were gradually suffocated by the new-comers.

It will be useful at this point to give some account of these Villanovans, who may stand as typical representatives of the native races encountered everywhere by the Etruscans, and who formed the real backbone and strength of their nation in after years.

The name is derived from the little hamlet of Villanova, eight kilometres from Bologna. There, as long ago as 1853, Count Gozzadini, an admirable archaeologist of the old school, discovered an important cremation cemetery containing tombs and antiquities of a kind never previously known in Italy. Excavations continued during the next sixty years, principally by Brizio and Zannoni, brought to light an entire chain of cemeteries all round Bologna, the output from which may be seen in the Museo Civico of that city. They extend over a chronological period which archaeologists estimate somewhat differently, but none would place at less than 300, and few at more than 500, years before the foundation of Etruscan Felsina. The whole civilization revealed in these cemeteries is on a much lower plane than the Etruscan. In the earliest of the three stages into which it is divided it is still almost within measurable distance of the Bronze Age; iron is scarce and rare, though bronze-working is well understood, and shows a perfect mastery of somewhat primitive processes. The rare decoration, which is used principally on pottery, is confined to the simple motives of that geometric school which was universal over the Balkans and Central Europe. In the second period, which centres on the eighth century, when Etruria was rapidly developing under the inspiration of its new masters, the Bolognese region remained almost unaffected by the new influence, and continued to develop its own barbaric civilization without any direct contact with the Etruscans. Its native arts and crafts were considerably improved and show noticeable progress at every point; but only an occasional object now and then betrays the influence of foreign motives beginning to percolate through, by the process of occasional barter and commerce. The cemeteries of the Villanovans still remained what they always had been, primarily transalpine, though towards the end of the period

Etruscan models begin to affect some details of the bronze work.

In the third period, which belongs to the seventh and sixth centuries, commercial intercourse between the north and south of the Apennines has become much more frequent. Even an occasional piece of Vetulonian jewellery is now found in the Villanovan tombs at Bologna. The increased output of the Etrurian mines shows its effect in the abundance of copper and bronze and a quite prodigal use of iron. In all branches of art and industry there are new developments; everywhere at Bologna it is evident that contact with a new and vitalizing school of foreign art is now affecting and slowly transforming the stubborn old native traditions, while leaving the groundwork of original custom untouched. But the northern Villanovans are still independent, not a single Etruscan has yet settled in their territory. And when about 500 B.C. the sudden aggression occurs by which an Etruscan colony is planted beside them, the Villanovans remain a distinct entity, retaining their own villages and their own burial grounds apart. Finally they disappear in the course of the fifth century, suffocated or driven away by the intrusive cuckoos, who were not long to survive them because they in turn were driven out by the Gauls.

At Bologna, then, we are able to study the character of this early civilization which precedes the Etruscan, without any of the interferences and disturbing factors which make it hard to unravel the tangled skeins south of the Apennines. We see a barbarian people which had descended from the Alps, coming probably from the Danube region in the eleventh century, and spreading down over the Romagna. Not content with this northern possession they pushed on, like their predecessors of the Bronze Age, over the Apennines down into Etruria and Latium, reaching the place where Rome was later to be founded and establishing themselves in the Alban hills. Partly the quest for agricultural lands and partly the lure of the copper-mines impelled them. Before the tenth century they had occupied the whole territory which the Etruscans were to conquer in the eighth. It is well, then, to estimate as far as possible the precise grade of civilization at which the Villanovans had arrived before the Etruscans fell in with them. They were a barbaric people, not to be compared in intellectual subtlety and finesse with the semi-Orientals who were to supplant them. Their dwellings were rude cabins, their settlements were small hamlets, they had none of the great traditions of civilized empires behind them. Some power of organization, however, they

must have had, such as even Zulus and rude
African peoples have often possessed, which en-
abled them to pursue a conquering march over
half the peninsula. But it is to be remembered
that the trail had been blazed for them by their
great-uncles of the Bronze Age, who had preceded them on the same route and subdued the
Neolithic peoples by the force of superior weapons.
Continuing to practise the simple crafts which they
had learned in their original homes in the Danube
valley, which rendered them as much superior to
the aborigines as the Etruscans were superior to
themselves, they arrived at a stage of civilization
which for a barbaric people must be considered
fairly high. Expert in the working of bronze,
capable iron-smiths, good manufacturers of simple
pottery, and practised to some extent in agriculture, they formed a population possessed of all the
qualities required to make a strong and progressive nation under capable leadership.

The leadership was supplied by the Etruscans, a
people of wholly different calibre and kind. These
Oriental immigrants had inherited the secular
fruits of Asiatic civilization. Born in lands where
agriculture was as old as the Garden of Eden, and
the traditions of the metal-workers went back to
Tubal Cain, they had become proselytes of the
Chaldaean priests and been touched with the

distant glamour of Egypt. In the ferment of new movements which had overthrown ancient empires they had probably taken their share. They had mingled with the artists of Tyre and Sidon, the warlike Hittites, the adventurous Greeks, the luxurious Lydians. Everything that could be learned from the melting-pot of the nearer East they had learned. And with this full equipment of knowledge, force, and experience, they came to organize and develop what the Villanovans had so well begun. By them the little village communities were united into cities, simple but well-built houses replaced the round cabins of wattle and clay. Religion was made an institution, temples were built, a hierarchical State was formed, and the community was divided into higher and lower orders.

A highly trained army, equipped with all the latest weapons, provided for the defence of the cities and made fresh conquests possible. The Villanovan land-lubber who had never seen a ship was taught the use of oars and sails, and no doubt pulled his weight in the galleys which brought merchandise to the newly built ports and fought the Phocaeans, Carthaginians, Syracusans, and any others who ventured into the Tyrrhene Sea. Engineering, hydraulics, building, and road-making, every application of contemporary science was applied, not perhaps in the first generation, but in the succeeding centuries, to the development of the rich province of Tuscany. Thus the way was prepared for the Roman, who, when he conquered Etruria in his turn, found a fully organized country at the highest point of material prosperity and wealth. The reasons why the Etruscans eventually failed to maintain their political control over a country which they had so wonderfully redeemed will be shown in the next chapter. As civilizing agents they were not merely the precursors of the Romans, they were the creators of a great part of ancient Italy.

Of the Etruscan excellence in the arts I have perhaps said enough, and have emphasized the independence of their creative genius to an extent which may not command universal assent. But their wonderful power of assimilation, their Japanese quickness of adaptation, must not be allowed to obscure the originality which shines out through all the borrowed trappings. The Etruscan borrowed much but he also originated much. The Roman borrowed everything, and it was very long before he began to originate.

The Villanovans were not the only people, though they were the chief, whom the Etruscans subdued in the course of their conquests in Italy. A vertical line drawn from Rimini, passing some distance to the west of Spoleto and ending at

Rome, will divide the pre-Etruscan population of South and Central Italy into two parts, on the basis of burial custom. Everything to the west of this line is cremation, everything to the east is inhumation. The cremating peoples are the Villanovans, those who practised inhumation were Umbrians and Picenes. In the first century, at least of Etruscan colonization, the settlements were confined to the west of the Apennines, and the earliest of all, as we have seen, were on the seacoast of the Tuscan Maremma. Etruria proper, the real Etruscan country of the Conquest, lies between the Arno on the north and the mouth of the Tiber on the south. But gradually incursions were made into the outlying Apennines on the east and even beyond this. Soon after the inland cities like Chiusi had been mastered the Etruscans crept on into what is now Umbria. How early Perugia was settled it is difficult to determine, but it was probably Etruscan by the sixth century. Even earlier than this there are distinct traces of Etruscan settlement in a tumulus at Fabriano in Picenum, but that part of the country has been so incompletely explored that it is impossible to draw wide conclusions. The Umbrians and the Picenes were of a totally distinct race-stock and origin from the Villanovans, and in many respects their civilization is quite different. They are probably descendants of the old Neolithic peoples who inhabited the country not only before the Villanovans entered it but even before their predecessors, the builders of the Terremare, came down in the Bronze Age.

The Umbrians eventually succumbed to the Etruscans, but the Picenes, who were exceptionally fine warriors, kept all intruders at bay. The Villanovans apparently had never dared to attack them, and so far as can be seen the Etruscans made very little progress on the East coast. It was not Etruscan but Ionian culture, acting through the mediation of Apulia, which eventually transformed the Picenes in the course of the sixth and fifth centuries.

In Campania, which they held only for a short time, the tribes which the Etruscans encountered were also of pre-Villanovan origin; though it is not certain whether they were in any way related to the peoples of the East coast. Here the Etruscan occupation left no lasting effects; the civilizing of the whole south of the peninsula fell inevitably to the Greeks. Nevertheless, though it is absurd to force Livy's words into a statement that there was an Etruscan empire stretching from the Alps to Messina it must be recognized that the Etruscans were the creators of more than a third of ancient Italy. A line from Milan to Chioggia and another from the mouth of the Po to the mouth of the Tiber would closely mark the limits of their permanent achievement. The sturdy peoples whom they led and by whom they were eventually assimilated were principally those who have survived into modern days as the Tuscans and the Umbrians.

CHAPTER 10

The collapse of the Etruscan power and its causes.

ABOUT the year 500 B.C. the Etruscan power was at its height, and the prospects of a unification of Italy at this early date seemed by no means remote. Etruria and Umbria had been consolidated into a uniform state, dominated by the twelve great cities and a number of minor towns. Latium had been so completely occupied as to be virtually an extension of Etruria beyond the Tiber. Outside this inner circle colonies had been pushed out northward into Romagna and the plains of the Po, southward into Campania. There seemed to be a fair chance that the southern half of the peninsula might be wrested from the Greeks; and as we look back it is hard to think that, with a little good fortune, the Etruscans might not have realized the dream of a single state stretching from the Alps to Messina. But suddenly the grip seems to relax, and their power crumbles almost with the swiftness of an ephemeral Oriental empire. Is not this phrase something more than an illustration? Was it not in the last analysis the latent Orientalism of their character that disqualified the Etruscans for founding a permanent and abiding state? On the other side there can be no doubt that it was nothing but the inflexible tenacity, the more than iron will of the Romans that gave them what the others could not win. The Etruscans had all the talents but one, the Romans had scarcely more than one; but it outweighed all the rest, and in the fullness of time, though very late in history, others were added to this one.

But if the fundamental causes of the fall of Etruria and the rise of Rome lie very deep, the external events which look like causes, though they are only the outward expression of the time spirit, are easy to describe and enumerate. The first military successes of the Etruscans are to be attributed quite as much to the absence of serious opposition as to any exceptional ability of their own. Cortes may have been a superman, but the Mexicans were very feeble opponents. Similarly, though the Villanovans were certainly inferior in arms and equipment, it must have been more than anything the absence of real coherence among the barbarians, scattered in their little village communities over a wide territory, that made them such easy victims of small but compact bands of spirited condottieri. If unified organized states existed anywhere in Italy at this time, which is very doubtful, they were to be found only in Venetia and Picenum, the very regions which the

Etruscans failed to penetrate. West of the Apennines we may infer that there was only disunion, caused principally by the survival of several distinct races which were averse to amalgamation. But Rome, when the fateful moment came, consolidated these tribes, welded them into a homogeneous material, and so forged the magic sword which must inevitably give victory to its possessor.

The expulsion of the Tarquins was really an event no less important than the Roman writers conceived it, though perhaps of a different character. It was the Italian declaration of Independence. The next move was directed by an imperative necessity; it was the reconstitution of the Latin League under Roman leadership. Strategically nothing could have been more perfectly designed to break the Etruscan power than the creation of a strong Latin state with its capital strongly entrenched on the lower Tiber. This drove a wedge into the heart of the newly formed Greater Etruria. The immediate effect was to split off Campania, which almost immediately fell into the hands of the expectant Greeks. These then proceeded to assure their safety on the seaward side by the naval victory of Cumae in 474 B.C. The battle of Cumae marked the beginning of a series of disasters for the Etruscan navy, now deprived of Carthaginian support as a result of the battle of Himera, and left unaided to face the vengeance of the Syracusans, who welcomed the opportunity to unite with their fellow Greeks of Campania. It was another phase of the world-war between Greek and Oriental; the Greeks were triumphant in every quarter. Hiero and his Syracusans dedicated at Olympia in memory of the battle of Cumae an Etruscan helmet, which is now in the British Museum, inscribed with a record of the event. Twenty years later the Syracusans captured Elba and Corsica, and sacked several ports on the Etruscan Maremma. It was like the thunder of the Dutch guns in the Medway in the time of Charles the Second.

In half a century the Etruscans had lost every yard of land south of the Tiber except the outpost of Fidenae, and their fleet had been reduced to impotence. But the heart of their territory remained intact. Etruria was untouched, and the young colonies north of the Apennines were flourishing. Moreover, if the Tyrrhene Sea was no longer theirs, the Adriatic offered a shorter route to Athens, now the principal goal of their commerce.

But the second phase of the struggle was already beginning, heralded by the duel between Veii and Rome. The fight with Veii was long and very bitter, as the Roman historians describe it, beginning about 480 and not ending till 396 B.C. The record may be read in the pages of Livy, and I do not propose to rehearse it here. What interests us for the philosophy of history is to observe how totally unnecessary it was that Veii should have been conquered, if only the Etruscans had been alive to the political and military situation. Here was a city so powerful and formidable that for fully eighty years it maintained a far from unequal struggle with Rome. Often Veii was temporarily victorious ; a very little aid would have made her success certain and final. But the Twelve Cities did not stir. Worse still, whilst the official Confederacy was totally apathetic the nearest neighbours, Caere, Tarquinia, Vulci, remained unmoved. If only one of the great cities of Southern Etruria had joined the Veientines, who had no allies except Capena and Falerii, the result could never have been doubtful. We can only say that Etruria committed suicide ; and can hardly pity those who suffered the results of such complete political incompetence. It was well for the world that the reins of power should pass to those who knew at least how to wield them. With the loss of Veii it was inevitable that Southern Etruria should be swallowed up piece by piece, and that the whole country up to the Arno should become Roman in a few generations. The conquest had been completed by the middle of the third century, in time to leave the Romans free to face Hannibal with their full strength in the second Punic War. Long before this the colonies of the Po valley had fallen before the invading Gauls, who burst down on them in the first years of the fourth century and converted what should have been new Etruria into Gallia Transpadana.

The failure of the Etruscans as empire builders is to be explained then principally by their inability or unwillingness to combine and co-operate for any common purpose. The Confederacy of the Twelve Cities, differently composed from time to time according to the varying fortunes of one or another member, must have been exceedingly loose in its organization to judge from its political inefficiency. Possibly it enforced few duties upon its members except those of a religious character. Certainly each city lived its own life, and conducted its own policy in peace and war with little regard for the wishes and interests of its neighbours. Caere could be on terms of cordial friendship with Rome while Veii was fighting for her life, and, all unrecognized, for the liberty of her fellow Etruscans. Tarquinia could stand coldly aloof alike from Rome and from Veii. If it had not been for the uniformity eventually imposed by Roman rule Etruria would soon have exhibited a picture not at all unlike that of Italy in general during the Middle Ages. A number of cities of markedly individual character would have developed their local civilization to the highest pitch, each under the independent rule of its own princely families. Etruria would have been no more a nation than Italy was a nation in the time of Dante. Perhaps it was at no time so much a nation as an aggregate of brilliant units, a series of beacons of art and beauty lit upon every hill-top in Tuscany. Those beacons were never extinguished though their light grew fainter under the Roman Empire. Sparks from the still glimmering fires were fanned into new flame centuries later by the Renaissance.

INDEX